Glossary of Grace

"Rhonda Kindig is clearly in love with the Bible and the God of grace revealed therein. With accessible (and whimsical) prose, she plumbs the evocative nuances of the original languages in brief reflections piquing curiosity for further word study. Newcomers to congregational life soon discover that signing on with Jesus sometimes feels like learning a whole new language. Kindig, a lifelong educator, is a trusty glossary guide toward faithfulness and fluency."

—**Frank G. Honeycutt**, author of *Death by Baptism: Sacramental Liberation in a Culture of Fear*

"Emily Dickenson said it best: 'I know nothing in the world that has as much power as a word.' Rhonda Kindig, in her biblical teaching and in this new book, concurs dramatically! Always the 'word' with her, whether Greek, Aramaic, or the King's English, she is the master at allowing students and her readers to discern Scripture's meaning through the word. We'll all be captivated by this one!"

—**Elizabeth S. Smith**, Assistant Professor of Music, Virginia Highlands Community College

"In *Glossary of Grace*, Rhonda Kindig turns would-be scholarly lectures into a spiritual conversation that proves both a comforting and an enlightening read. Through her fascination with words and the Word of God, plus her extensive knowledge of Hebrew, Greek, and Latin, these essays not only enrich an understanding of biblical vocabulary but also bring to light abundant examples of God's grace."

—**Bonny Gable**, contributing editor, *A! Magazine for the Arts*

"Rhonda Kindig is a gifted student of the languages of the Scriptures, but above all, she is a teacher. She interprets the biblical language so that we can connect with each other and with God. She helps us delve into the spiritual depths of truth about God in her fifty-one explorations of major biblical terms. She gives them context with a surprisingly short and rich explanation that is easily understood. *Glossary of Grace* is a must for everyone's library."

—**Emily Edmondson**, Rector, Christ Episcopal Church,
Marion, Virginia

"Once again Rhonda Kindig has given us her unique combination of faith, scholarship, and devotion in *Glossary of Grace*. This book makes esoteric terms understandable. As one who regularly interacts with 'readers' in Bible study, Kindig always connects in a personal way. It is her gift; thanks be to God!"

—**James Bangle**, retired Lutheran Pastor

Glossary of Grace

Rhonda Karen Kindig

RESOURCE *Publications* · Eugene, Oregon

GLOSSARY OF GRACE

Resource Publications
An Imprint of Wipf and Stock Publishers
199 W. 8th Ave., Suite 3
Eugene, OR 97401

www.wipfandstock.com

PAPERBACK ISBN: 978-1-6667-1798-3
HARDCOVER ISBN: 978-1-6667-1799-0
EBOOK ISBN: 978-1-6667-1800-3

08/16/21

Contents

CONTENTS

Introduction

The goal of this volume is to offer an accessible glossary of approximately fifty key biblical terms. Unlike ordinary dictionaries, this glossary offers concise devotional essays to explain each concept. In addition to finding useful definitions for the selected words, the reader will find an underlying theme of God's grace shining through every page. Whether used as needed to seek explanations of theological terms, for either personal study or classroom use, or read in sequence as a devotional volume, it is hoped that "Glossary of Grace" will fulfill your needs while underscoring the abundant grace of God. Thanks be to God!

Agape Love

Simon, son of John, do you love me? —John 21:15-17

You surely have noticed that acronyms are infiltrating our language, thanks to the lightning speed of texting. Our communication is becoming streamlined by this shorthand. LOL means laugh out loud; BFF means best friends forever, BTW means by the way.

In the twenty-first chapter of John, Jesus asks Peter three times if he loves him. Did you realize that Peter's reply all three times is, essentially, that he is Jesus' BFF? When we read this conversation, we are in blissful ignorance of the fact that Greek has three different words for love. Physical, romantic love is *eros*; brotherly love is *philia* (as in Philadelpia, city of brotherly love); charitable, unconditional, divine love is *agape.* Jesus is using *agape* love the first two times he asks; Peter uses *philia* all three times!

Jesus' invitation is for us to recognize and announce OMG, in the only appropriate use for that acronym! Just one chapter later in John's gospel, disciple Thomas will make that very pronouncement. Thomas will be the first one in recorded history to say to Jesus, "My Lord and my God!" (John 20:28). We do Thomas a disservice nicknaming him "Doubting"; he should be "Proclaiming Thomas"!

> God's love has been poured into our hearts through the
> Holy Spirit that has been given to us. (Rom 5:5)

From our earliest days, we've probably associated God with love, perhaps beginning with the sweet song, "Jesus loves me, this I know for the Bible tells me so." Paul's statement in Romans is not at all surprising. The verb phrase, "poured out" instantly is recognizable as the action of cleansing and new life that we clearly identify with baptism. Actually, it is also an Old Testament verb.

Paul is subtly announcing that God's saving designs had already been revealed in the Hebrew Scriptures. Here are some examples of prophecies about the Spirit streaming downward from heaven to give new life to the world:

> I will pour out water upon the thirsty ground . . .
> I will pour out my spirit upon your offspring. (Isa 44:3)
>
> I will pour out my spirit upon all flesh. (Joel 3:1)
>
> I will sprinkle clean water over you . . . I will give you a new heart, and a new spirit I will put within you. (Ezek 36:25–26)

Lots of New Testament references speak about the pouring out of the Spirit. What is interesting is that Paul has given a new twist to the concept. Romans 5:5 is the only place in all of scripture in which love (*agape*) is poured out on us! He has made the leap that recognizes the Holy Spirit is the gift of love.

For the Bible tells me so! Thanks be to God!

Apocalypse

This word simply means "revelation"; it comes directly from the Greek, *apocalypsis*. It means an unveiling, a pulling back of a curtain. Think of the scene in the movie "*The Wizard of Oz*", when the dog Toto pulls back the curtain to reveal the wizard is an ordinary man! If you are a fan of home renovation programs, the final "big reveal" is an apocalypse. The word was never intended to mean a cataclysmic end of the world. Think of all the ways God has revealed himself throughout the biblical narratives.

An apocalypse may seem frightening, but it is usually presented as a cautionary tale. An author (such as Daniel, John of Patmos, or Matthew) takes an event from the past (i.e., the destruction of the Temple), and predicts it as something to occur in the future, in order to warn his audience of a situation they are enduring (i.e., Roman occupation). To show how this works, consider the chart below.

The idea is to remind the audience that just as God acted in the past, as in delivering his people from bondage, restoring his people who were exiled, to remembering his people when they are lost, we can rely on God to set things right for us. Thanks be to God!

APOCALYPTIC TENSE

To warn his audience about a current concern

A writer takes an event from the past

Predicts the event in the future

Atonement/Day of Atonement/ Yom Kippur

Atonement is an English word we find used in the Old Testament as well as the New Testament, but interestingly the English word was not coined until the sixteenth century. William Tyndale, an English translator of the Bible, created the word to translate the Latin "reconciliatio." This word atonement is unique in that it does not come from one of the original languages of the Bible.

The actual meaning of Tyndale's word is easy to deduce, as it is a compound of sorts: "at one + ment", or being reconciled to God. Some translations of the Bible still rely on "reconciliation" rather than Tyndale's word.

In the New Testament, the word is used exclusively in the life, death, and resurrection of Jesus. The apostle Paul was a fan of the concept, which he explains in Romans:

> But now, apart from law, the righteousness of God has been disclosed, and is attested by the law and the prophets, the righteousness of God through faith in Jesus Christ for all who believe. For there is no distinction, since all have sinned and fall short of the glory of God, they are now justified by his grace as a gift, through the redemption that is in Christ Jesus, whom God put forward as a sacrifice of atonement by his blood, effective through faith. (Rom 3:21–25)

In the Old Testament, the Hebrew word that is translated as atonement can be rendered by a number of words: "cleanse", "expiate", "purify", "purge". We find in Old Testament scripture that offerings and sacrifices were atoning, all of which had to be carried out by the high priests.

For Jews, atonement means the same thing as for Christians, being "at one" with God, but they believe it is attained differently. Christians, because of the sinful nature of humanity, believe that any atonement comes from God, through the sacrificial death of Christ Jesus. That is to say, we are in bondage to sin and cannot free ourselves. It is God's gracious gift that enables us to be "at one" with God. The Jews believe that since sins are actions done by them, they must be absolved by actions taken by them.

In the Old Testament, we read of *Yom Kippur,* the Day of Atonement (Lev 16). On that one day each year, the high priest would enter the Holy of Holies, the innermost sanctum of the Tabernacle or Temple, and splash sacrificial blood on the altar and the cover (*kapporeth*) of the Ark of the Covenant. In addition, the entire sin of all the people for the past year was symbolically placed upon a sacrificial goat that was then driven into the wilderness, taking the body of sin with it. Hence, we have the term, *scapegoat*!

Today observant Jews spend the Day of Atonement in fasting and repenting. A Jew rights his wrongs by confessing and pledging to go forward, sinning no more.

Modern Christians also repent and confess, but we have the sacrament of Holy Communion, in which we hear the words of Jesus spoken at the Last Supper, and we are assured that we are granted atonement. Thanks be to God!

Barren Woman Tradition

Then God remembered Rachel. —Gen 30:22

[Hannah] made this vow: "O LORD of hosts, if only you
will look on the misery of your servant, and remember
me, and not forget your servant, but will give to your
servant a male child, then I will set him before you."
—1 Sam 1:11

In the Bible, the theme of special birth circumstances surfaces so
frequently that it has a name, the *barren woman tradition*. Women
who remain barren for years suddenly give birth to a very special
child. From the Old Testament, we could name Samuel's mother,
Hannah, who was quite old, but she prayed to God for child and
was given one at last. We remember that Samson's mother had been
barren for years and years. In the New Testament, Elizabeth, the
mother of John the Baptist, was advanced in age, too.

Special births, in the Bible and other traditions, portend the
importance or uniqueness of the child born. For example, many
believed Julius Caesar was destined to be great because he was
born by Caesarean section (hence the term). Of course, Mary
of Nazareth, the mother of Jesus, had the most unusual circum-
stance of all.

In Genesis, the matriarch Sarah had been barren a lifespan;
Isaac was born when she was in her nineties. Her situation was so
extreme (being beyond menopause) that the prophet Isaiah used
her as an example to encourage the Jewish people during their exile
to "keep the faith". Later, Isaac's wife, Rebekah, despaired that she
remained barren many years. When she finally did become preg-
nant, she suffered dreadfully as the twins, Esau and Jacob, struggled
mightily in the womb. In the next generation after that, Jacob's wife

Rachel, too, remained barren for years, while pining with jealousy at the children her own sister Leah continued to birth with Jacob. Ultimately, Rachel gave birth to Joseph, who would grow to be a savior of his people, but her happiness did not last long; she died during the childbirth of her second son.

So, why is the barren woman tradition archetypical in Genesis? It shows the precariousness of our existence and our dependence upon God. Genesis clearly claims that God "remembered" each of these barren women. Every time the future seems about to be extinguished, God "remembers", whether it be a barren woman or a covenant with the people. Our very existence . . . as a family, as a race, as individuals . . . has always depended upon God's memory. Thanks be to God!

Bless and Curse

> If you will only obey the LORD your God, by diligently observing all his commandments that I am commanding you today,
>
> . . . all these blessings shall come upon you and overtake you, if you obey the LORD your God.
>
> . . . But if you will not obey the LORD your God by diligently observing all his commandments and decrees, which I am commanding you today, then all these curses shall come upon you and overtake you.
>
> —Deut 28:1–2, 15

These verses are from the instructions Moses gave the Israelites for how the covenant with God would be ratified as soon as they crossed the River Jordan into the promised land of Canaan. Half of the tribes of Israel were to ascend Mt. Ebal, while the other half of the tribes would ascend Mt. Gerizim. Then a detailed list of blessings and curses were to be shouted out across the valley, with the people all shouting "Amen." According to Joshua 8:30–35, the ceremony did take place, with all the men, women, and children participating.

The blessings and curses applied to either following or not following the covenant with God. Contrary to our modern understanding of "curse", the curses are not a description of divine punishment for disobeying the commands, and neither are the blessings rewards for compliance. The Hebrew word *barak*, that is translated as "bless", literally means to "kneel down". This suggests that *barak* involves offering something or doing something for another. *Barak* means that God will provide for our needs.

Think of the child-rearing advice of the 1990s, to use natural and logical consequences rather than punishments and rewards to motivate children toward appropriate behavior. God, our Father, has given the gift of instructions for harmonious living. If we follow this way of life, we can be assured that we are serving God. If we elect to disregard the instructions, our contrary behavior tends to set into motion results, or consequences, that are not harmonious. Such disharmony can have long-reaching impact, but God does not cause it or desire it.

The words in Deuteronomy chapters 27 and 28 may remind you of Jesus' sermon from Luke 6:20–26. The "blessed are you" and "woe to you" listings that Jesus offers are, again, statements describing natural consequences. They most certainly are not proclamations actively separating people into camps of ever-lasting salvation versus eternal damnation. "Blessed," as used here in Luke, is a description and not a prediction. "Woe" is simply a word that means "Alas!" Benedictions and maledictions are descriptions of how things are. God desires to shower his blessings upon his children. Let's not be contrary children, causing God to say, "Alas!" Thanks be to God!

Covenant

> I will establish my covenant between me and you, and
> your offspring after you throughout their generations,
> for an everlasting covenant, to be God to you and to
> your offspring after you. —Gen 17:7

In story after story in the book of Genesis, we encounter flawed
characters and dysfunctional families. Indeed, the persistence of
human sin might be the most permeating motif throughout the
Bible. "If we say we have no sin, we deceive ourselves and the truth
is not in us" (1 John 1:8–9). But if sin is ubiquitous in the Bible, so
is God's activity in dealing with it.

In story after story, beginning in the book of Genesis, the
testimony of the Bible is that God approaches individuals to enter into relationship. The term for this divine/human relationship
is *covenant.*

There are many biblical examples of alliances between humans, including contracts, treaties, and marriages. The Hebrew
word for covenant originally meant "shackle" or "chain". But the
biblical concept of covenant as relationship with God is something
new and marvelous. The novel element is that mortal humans
would be bound into a relationship in which God, the Creator of
the Universe, is a party in the promises. For the Jewish people, the
covenant with God introduced in Genesis is *Berit Olam,* which
translates as "Everlasting Covenant".

We find a foundation for covenant in God's three-fold promise to Abram (Abraham) in Genesis 12:2–3: "I will make of you
a great nation, and make your name great, so that you will be a
blessing . . . in you all the families of the earth shall be blessed." As
we keep reading in Genesis, each of these promises is elevated to a
covenant, which we find fulfilled later in scripture.

The promise of nationhood, ratified in Genesis 15, we see fulfilled in the Mosaic Covenant, when the "family" is forged into a nation during its experiences under Moses' leadership in the wilderness for forty years. The promise of a great name, ratified in Genesis 17, will be fulfilled in the Davidic Covenant, the continuation of King David's dynasty. The promise of worldwide blessing, ratified in Genesis 22, comes to fruition with the New Covenant, which is the universal blessing poured out with Christ's blood.

> I hereby make a covenant. Before all your people I will perform marvels, such as have not been performed in all the earth or in any nation, and all the people among whom you live shall see the work of the LORD; for it is an awesome thing that I will do with you. —Exod 34:10

So, two little Hebrew words, *Berit Olam*, summarize all of God's saving action, and we are confident that God's promise, this covenant, is valid in perpetuity. For ever and ever. Amen. Thanks be to God!

Day of the Lord

Multiple texts in the Hebrew Bible express the absolute conviction that God will put things right for God's people. An example of this is in the *Song of Deborah*, from Judges 5, which is recognized as the very oldest portion of scripture. The Judges passage includes words like *triumphs, victories, righteous acts,* and *blessings*. It is this very belief in God's ultimate victory that underlies the original Day of the Lord concept. It describes God's vindication, when God would put things right through his own means.

By the time of the prophetic writings, when folks like Amos were unsure whether the Israelites could keep the responsibilities of being in covenant with God, the Day of the Lord came to mean a time of separating good from bad: "Alas, for you who desire the day of the LORD! . . . It is darkness, not light" (Amos 5:18).

We need to recapture the mood from Deborah's song of deliverance, in which absolutely all are convinced of God setting everything right again. Most people nowadays view the coming Day of the Lord as a dire Judgment Day when people will get "their just desserts". An ancient rabbinic tradition suggests, instead, that any separation of bad from good will be from within the hearts of each individual.

We must not become the judges ourselves. God's justice is not ours. God's justice is not retributive (an eye for an eye). God's justice is distributive (blessings for all)!

Then what is God's wrath? Doesn't that suggest anger and punishment? Actually, the Greek word *(orgos)* is much like our word urge. It simply means a reaction or response to something. Here's how it works: God is holy, so absolutely anything and everything that is unholy is deflected away from the holiness of God.

Rather than an emotion, like rage, wrath is a deflection of unholiness from the Holy One.

In John 12:31, we read, "Now is the judgment of this world." What might that tell us about the coming Day of the Lord? Could it have already happened . . . once and for all . . . on a Good Friday just about two millennia ago?

Perhaps a reassuring understanding for the coming Day of the Lord would focus on the "coming" part—it is God who is ever and forever coming toward us with gracious gifts of redemption, reconciliation, and restoration. Thanks be to God!

Election/Rejection/Repentance/Restoration

> They are Israelites, and to them belong the adoption, the glory, the covenants, the giving of the law, the worship, and the promises; to them belong the patriarchs and from them, according to the flesh, comes the Messiah, who is over all, God blessed forever. Amen.
> —Rom 9:4–5

The apostle Paul loved his kinfolk—the Jews, or Israelites. Indeed, the verse above shows all the advantages, the irrevocable promises, they have been given by God. In the earlier chapters of Romans, Paul argued that God treated Jews and Gentiles with the same righteousness and grace, so why does he still persist in identifying two separate categories of people and stressing the benefits the Israelites have been given?

It troubles Paul greatly that the bulk of Israel has not responded favorably to the gospel of Christ Jesus. In chapters 9 through 11 in Romans, Paul wrestles with Israel's election by God, followed their rejection of the Messiah, but offering hope for their restoration ultimately.

There are multiple examples in the Old Testament of the people rejecting God's gifts and then being offered reconciliation with God. Shortly after God delivered the people from their bondage in Egypt, they rejected God by worshipping a golden calf. After forty years of relying solely on God's manna economy, a new generation entered the promised land. Later, after years of idolatry during the reigns of Israel's and Judah's kings, both kingdoms are conquered, and the people are driven from their homeland. After seventy years of exile, a remnant was allowed to return to rebuild

Jerusalem. At another time, prophet Jonah received a divine commission to preach to the great city of Nineveh; instead, he headed the opposite direction to Tarshish. After storms at sea and becoming the dinner of a "big fish", Jonah repents and goes successfully to Nineveh. The book of Judges, also, shows a dozen instances of a cycle of rejection followed by repentance and then restoration. The people did "what was evil in the sight of the Lord" (Judg 2:11), but later they cried out for help, and a deliverer, like Gideon or Deborah, was sent. So, Paul's pattern, in chapters 9 through 11, is nothing new for the Bible.

It is exactly this continual restoration offered by God that encourages Paul about the situation with the Jews' rejection of Jesus as Messiah. What seems obvious, then, is that the cycle is between rejection and restoration only, because election (being "chosen" by God) is not cyclical. Rather, it is a constant, underlying all of the Biblical narratives. Keep in mind that this is not God's showing of favoritism for the Israelites. They were not elected as the sole object of God's love. No, they were selected to be instruments of God's love. Indeed, God's call to Abraham was that through him "all the families of the earth shall be blessed" (Gen 12:3).

Thanks be to God!

Eschatology

A prevalent Jewish worldview in the first century was based on an expectation for an end of the current age. There was a dichotomy between the era in which they lived and the promise of a world-to-come. Jewish scriptures are full of this expectation, which they called *ha olam habah*.

Eschatology is the study of final things. The Greek word, *eschaton*, means "last things". This is not so much a consideration of the end of the world, as it is a conclusion to a present era, in order that a new one might be ushered in.

Our current era, this world, is ruled by sin and death. The *ha olam habah* is a new creation, based on a new covenant.

For the apostle Paul, this has already been begun. In Christ Jesus, there is an in-breaking of heavenly realities. We live with one foot in the old creation already here, but with the other foot in the "not yet", the world-to-come. Imagine a Venn diagram, with two overlapping circles. The circle on the left represents the Old Covenant, or the Present Age. This is where we already exist. The circle on the right stands for the New Covenant, or the World-to-Come. This suggests the time that is "not yet". The overlap in the middle illustrates those who are "in Christ".

It is the death and resurrection of Jesus Christ that ushers in the new age. We, the baptized, are already living "in Christ", already able to experience the new covenant in his blood, the intersection of the old world with the world-to-come. Thanks be to God!

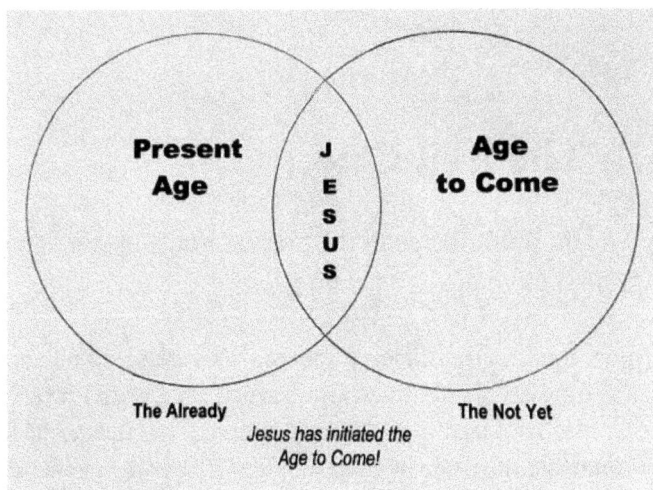

Jesus has initiated the
Age to Come!

Evil/The Evil One

> And do not bring us to the time of trial, but rescue us
> from the evil one. —Matt 6:13

This more modern translation might make us wonder a bit about a previous translation. You may have learned the Lord's Prayer with these words: "And lead us not into temptation, but deliver us from evil." You may think there is quite a difference between general evil and an evil one. The newer translation suggests there is some sort of embodiment of evil, such as a devil, which is a real threat.

The original Greek text can actually be translated either way. The Greek language lacked indefinite articles (*a, an*); they could never say "an" evil, or "a" wicked one. However, the language was ripe with definite articles. In fact, every Greek noun was always paired in speech and writing with the definite article, which is "*the.*"

English speakers would not usually include the definite article with abstract nouns, such as love, courage, truth, or evil; Greek speakers would. Therefore, to translate the Greek passage from Matthew, *tou ponerou*, the translator has a choice. Did Matthew intend "evil", as in evil in general, or was "the evil (one)" intended?

In this particular petition of the Lord's Prayer, either way works, of course, but in your personal understanding, it is up to your imagination to decide which is more fitting phrase. Matthew intends that we be delivered from any and all *tou ponerou.* Thanks be to God!

Feast or Festival of Passover (Pesah)

Passover may be the most familiar of Jewish holidays for Christians, as we know its relationship to the life of Jesus.

It is a spring-time festival (from the first to the fifteenth of the month of Nisan). The institution of Passover can be read about in the twelfth chapter of Exodus. During the ultimate plague inflicted upon Pharaoh, all the first-born of the land were to die. The Israelites were "passed over" by following the instructions from God, involving special preparation of a lamb and the painting of lamb's blood upon the lintels of their doors. Thus began their liberation from bondage in Egypt.

For Jews, Passover is a celebration not just for commemoration of their redemption from slavery in Egypt but also in anticipation of future redemption.

It is a feast of participation. The people are to re-experience the bondage and liberation that is part of their story; it is more than just a memory of what ancient people experienced.

A central tradition to Passover is the seder meal, a re-living of the original Passover meal, with symbolic foods. It is a family ritual, emphasizing the story for all generations.

The mandate for celebrating Passover is found in Leviticus 23. It is one of the three major pilgrimage festivals for which all able-bodied men had to journey to the Temple in Jerusalem. Luke's gospel includes a story of twelve-year-old Jesus going up for the Passover with his parents (Luke 2:41–52).

The gospel of John gives a detailed chronology for the last week of Jesus' life, including the approaching Passover. In John's gospel, the crucifixion of Jesus occurs on the Day of Preparation for Passover, on which the blemish-free, one-year-old lambs were sacrificed.

It is in John's gospel that connections are drawn to Jesus being our new "Lamb of God" (John 1:36). For evangelist John, Jesus is the embodiment of the Paschal Lamb. Thanks be to God!

Feast or Festival of Pentecost or Weeks (Shavuot)

The word "Pentecost" is Greek, referring to "fifty days". It refers to the festival of Shavuot celebrating the gift from God of the *Torah* (the Teachings). The Torah showed the people how to live in this world as people set apart in relationship to God and each other.

The Bible does not give us a link between Shavuot and Sinai, but the giving of the commandments at Mt. Sinai, fifty days after the deliverance from bondage in Egypt, is the tradition underlying the commemoration. (See Exodus chapters 19 and 20.) At that time, the entire people had a theophany of the Voice of the Divine speaking to them. Shavuot is considered an experience shared by all Jews for all time. In other words, the belief is that every individual heard that Voice!

Shavuot, also called the Feast of Weeks, is another harvest festival, celebrating first-fruits. Instructions for this are given in the twenty-third chapter of Leviticus.

The Jews do not commemorate with a re-creation of the Sinai event, instead all Jews are called to remember and re-affirm commitment to the Torah and its study. This is to be a continuous renewal rather than an annual re-enactment.

It is on the day of Pentecost, according to Luke's second book, Acts of the Apostles, that the Holy Spirit came to the disciples gathered in Jerusalem. As tongues of flame appeared above their heads, they began to speak in languages that all the crowd from around the Mediterranean were able to understand. Simon Peter delivered a sermon that day after which three thousand people were baptized. (See Acts 2:1–42.)

So, for Jews, Pentecost was a festival of re-commitment to the Torah, and for Christians Pentecost became the birthday of the church. Thanks be to God!

Feast or Festival of Tabernacles or Booths (Sukkot)

We learn about this Jewish festival in the twenty-third chapter of Leviticus. It was an ancient agricultural time associated with ingathering, just before winter. It was one of the three annual festivals so important that every able-bodied Jewish man had to make a pilgrimage to the Temple in Jerusalem.

Sukkot is also called the Feast of Tabernacles or Booths, because of the huts (called *sukkah*) people are to make to live in and eat in during the seven days (from the fifteenth to the twenty-first of the month of Tishri), recalling the tents the Israelites lived in during the forty years of wandering in the wilderness after the exodus from Egypt. It might also be related to living in temporary huts beside agricultural fields during a harvest or ingathering.

King Solomon consecrated the Temple during Sukkot (1 Kings 8). Sukkot is a festival that looks to the future. We read in Zechariah 14:16 that during Sukkot all nations will come to Jerusalem to rejoice during the future Messianic time.

According to the seventh chapter of John's gospel, Jesus goes to the Temple during the Festival of Booths. An elaborate water ritual was performed each of the seven days by the priests. While pouring golden pitchers full of water over the altar, they offered prayers for restoration, with an expectation that the rivers that had watered the Garden of Eden would burst forth from the altar right there in the Temple. It was at this time that Jesus began to speak of rivers of living water and claiming that he is the new altar from which living water flows. Thanks be to God!

First Fruits

If the part of the dough, offered as first fruits is holy,
then the whole batch is holy; and if the root is holy,
then the branches also are holy. —Rom 11:16

In the middle of Paul's explanation to the Romans about what will become of those Jews who do not believe that Jesus is the Messiah, he offers an Old Testament concept known as "first fruits". The idea is that when a harvest is successful, the first fruits are brought as a sacrificial offering to God. These first are a representative of the whole, which God had given to the farmer, and the farmer offers these back to God in thanksgiving for the whole harvest.

This ritual of thanksgiving extends beyond the harvest. In Numbers 15:17–21, we read, "After you come into the land to which I am bringing you, whenever you eat of the bread of the land, you shall present a donation to the LORD. From your first batch of dough you shall present a donation to the LORD."

The tradition extends even further back into the Old Testament. When plagues are sent against Egypt in the story of the Exodus, the final plague involves the deaths of the firstborn throughout the land. The firstborn of the Israelites are spared, because they marked their doorframes with blood from Passover lambs. In thanksgiving, the Israelite firstborn are thereafter to be consecrated to the Lord (Exod 13).

Just as a remnant stands for a whole, so the first fruits stand for the whole harvest. Just as Israel was elected by God (not as the sole object of God's love but as the instrument of God's love), Israel was destined to be a blessing to all nations.

And as we think about how a part or remnant can carry forward the promises to a greater whole, there is another such comparison that underlies the New Testament, and that is the message of Easter. Jesus Christ is the "first fruits" of the resurrected. What good news for us, the whole of creation, that we are the "whole harvest" to follow! Thanks be to God!

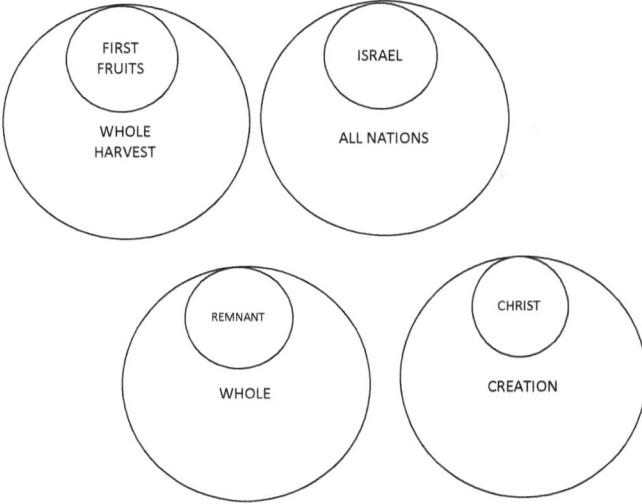

Glory/Glorification

> It is that very Spirit bearing witness with our spirit that we are children of God, and if children, then heirs of God and joint heirs with Christ. If, in fact, we suffer with him so that we may also be glorified with him. —Rom 8:16–17

> The glory that you have given me I have given them, so that they may be one, as we are one, I in them and you in me, that they may be completely one, so that the world may know that you have sent me and have loved them even as you have loved me. —John 17:22–23

Is that not an incredible idea? That we may also attain glorification! The eighth chapter of Romans is a turning point in the letter to the Romans, with the idea of the adoption of the baptized as brothers and sisters with Christ Jesus. Earlier in Romans, Paul had written, "We boast in our hope of sharing the glory of God" (Rom 5:2). From the two quoted verses, it is not clear whether this shared glorification is something for our present time or the future. It is clear that we are to follow the path of the crucified Messiah in this life.

So, first we might ask just what is this "glory"? The Greek word *doxa*, as in doxology, and the Hebrew *Shekinah*, which are translated into "glory", refer to the Very Presence of God. For Moses, this glory was so great that after he'd been in the presence for forty days, he had to wear a veil before the Israelites, because his face shone so very brilliantly. According to Exodus 40:34, the tabernacle was where the *Shekinah*, the Very Presence of God, would dwell in the midst of the people. Later, this Glory of the LORD resided in Solomon's Temple (1 Kings 8:1). In Psalm 63:2, we read, "I have looked upon the sanctuary, beholding your power and glory."

Our adoption, however, is not into a life of ease without troubles. You've heard the phrase, "No pain, no gain." Well, it follows, "No suffering, no glory!" Our path to glorification follows that of the crucified Jesus, steps into a world that is inundated with misery and suffering. How can we manage that? If we hope to bear the image of Christ, we must be conformed to the image of Christ crucified. It is the life of love poured out for others. It is nothing less than our participation in the divine life, and it begins in this life right now.

Paul wrote in his letter to the Corinthians, "All of us with unveiled faces, seeing the glory of the Lord . . . are being transformed into the same image from one degree of glory to another; for this comes from the Lord, the Spirit" (2 Cor 3:18). Here's good news—the Holy Spirit walks with us this cruciform path. Thanks be to God!

Grace

The grace of our Lord Jesus Christ be with you.
—Rom 16:20

If you are looking in Hebrew in the Old Testament, finding a word that exactly translates as grace might take you some time. The word that most encapsulates grace is rendered into English as mercy, or loyalty, or goodness, or favor, or even lovingkindness, a word coined by Bible translator Miles Coverdale in 1535. But that lovingkindness in the Hebrew Bible is never used to describe anything between humans; it is always offered to describe God's steadfastness and persistence in his love for his covenant people. It is God's *hesed* (that's the Hebrew) that will not let Israel go, despite Israel's continual waywardness. The Psalms sing of this regularly. Other Old Testament texts sing of it as well:

> The LORD, the LORD, a God merciful and gracious,
>
> Slow to anger, and abounding in steadfast love
>
> And faithfulness,
>
> Keeping steadfast love for the thousandth generation,
>
> Forgiving iniquity and transgression and sin.
> (Exod 34:6–7)

In the third century BC, when the Hebrew Bible was first translated into Greek, the *hesed* became *eleos* (mercy or pity). Later, when Jerome wrote a Latin translation in the fourth century AD, he used the term *misericordia* (merciful). Thankfully, our English translations have tried to be more faithful to the full weight of *hesed*. When you read "steadfast love" in the Old Testament, you come closer to the fuller meaning, which is a composite of love with strength and fidelity.

Now for the Greek in the New Testament. The Greek for grace is *charis*. Interestingly, as a gift, this is *charisma* (sound familiar?). The most literary definition for grace is as a gift. What do we know about gifts? The best are given with joy. How amazing that the Greek word for joy is *chara/chaira!*

When Martin Luther was writing the German translation of the Bible, in the 1530s, he translated both the Hebrew *hesed* and the Greek *charis* into the same German word, *gnade*. And, *gnade* is German for grace. That's how grace became our word.

Paul's letters give us the most uses of grace in the New Testament. Indeed, it is Paul who develops the concept most fully for us.

> For I am convinced that neither death, nor life, nor angels, nor rulers, nor things present, nor things to come, nor powers, nor height, nor depth, nor anything else in all creation, will be able to separate us from the love of God in Christ Jesus our Lord. (Romans 8:38–39)

Thanks be to God!

Grace and Peace

> Grace to you and peace from God our Father and the
> Lord Jesus Christ. —Gal 1:3

These familiar words open just about every letter written by the apostle Paul. Indeed, the words may be so familiar that we do not take time to consider the theological depth in them! Reformer Martin Luther boldly claimed that it was these two key words, *grace* and *peace*, which make up Christianity.

Interestingly, these two pillars can also be found in the Old Testament. An ancient blessing reads:

> The LORD bless you and keep you; the LORD make his
> face to shine upon you and be gracious to you; the LORD
> lift up his countenance upon you and give you peace.
> (Num 6:24–26)

Notice that in the blessing from the Numbers, we do not see the word *grace* but rather *gracious*. As an adjective describing God, the word *gracious* appears numerous times in the Old Testament, but the noun *grace* is not an Old Testament word. On the other hand, in the New Testament, *grace* abounds. We might even consider that *grace* is the embodiment of the *gracious* God.

A gracious God is the main character of the Old Testament, while the New Testament presents God incarnated as Jesus Christ, who bestows grace so abundantly.

We learn in the Old Testament that the "law" was the gift of the covenant to God's people. The law taught the way to live a holy life, a life set apart as people of God. The law was a way to align oneself with God and others, to bring harmony and peace.

The law, however, is not able to release us from our sinful human nature. The good news of the New Testament is that through

Christ's sacrificial death on the cross, we have been brought into alignment with God. That is the gift of grace.

So, when we read or hear "grace and peace to you," we are truly hearing Christianity in a nutshell. Thanks be to God!

$$
\begin{array}{ccccc}
& & G & & \\
& & R & & \\
P & E & A & C & E \\
& & C & & \\
& & E & &
\end{array}
$$

Hell/Hades/Sheol

Is hell a frightening concept for you? Do you believe there is a geographical location where an angry God banishes the damned for eternity? What does the Bible say about this? Surprisingly little, actually!

Jewish theology from the Hebrew Bible, which is our Old Testament, does not include either heaven or hell as ultimate destinations. As for the New Testament, the word appears less than a dozen times in the four Gospels and zero times in Revelation.

The English word is a rendering of the Hebrew place name *ge-hinnom,* which means the Valley of Hinnom, or Gehenna. Gehenna was south of Jerusalem and was a place of infamy during the times of the monarchs of Judah. It was a place where idolatrous practices occurred, as well as human sacrifice. By the time of Jesus, Gehenna had become a horrid rubbish heap, where all manner of filth, dead animals, and even corpses of evil-doers were thrown. To avoid outbreaks of pestilence from all the rotting carcasses, fires were kept burning constantly. Imagine the stench!

From pagan fire rituals to garbage dump, Gehenna was an abominable place that became a metaphor for damnation. Often, Gehenna was translated from Hebrew into the Greek word *Hades.* If you are familiar with Greek mythology, Hades was the name of the underworld deity, and it later became the name for that domain, a place of no-return for those who had died. It was associated with the finality of death.

In the Hebrew Bible, however, the dead were just imagined to be in a shadowy place called *Sheol,* or the Pit. It was not a place for punishment, it was just the final location for all the dead. Another euphemism found in the Hebrew Bible for death was "sleeping with ones ancestors." "Then David slept with his ancestors" (1 Kings 2:10). Perhaps that is the basis for "eternal rest".

The word *hell* comes to our English language from Anglo-Saxon pagan ritual. The modern concept of hell as a fiery place of torture and agony comes to us more from Dante's fourteenth century writing, *The Inferno*, than from the Bible! Add to that ideas from Milton's seventeenth century book, *Paradise Lost*, and you have the primary sources for the contemporary culture's horrible place where sinners descend upon death.

Nothing about such an understanding meshes with God's promises and intentions for his creation, as we find in a faithful reading of the Bible. What we find at the core of the New Testament is Emmanuel, God-with-us, entering into all suffering with us, ever-and-always extending his love, offering us hope "once for all" in the Holy Week story. Thanks be to God!

Jealous/Zealous God

You shall not bow down to them or worship them; for
I the LORD your God am a jealous God. —Exod 20:5

For you shall worship no other god, because the LORD,
whose name is Jealous, is a jealous God. —Exod 34:14

For the LORD your God is a devouring fire, a jealous God.
—Deut 4:24

The green-eyed monster! To our ears, jealousy is not a compliment. It is borderline envy, which, according to Roman Catholic tradition going back to Pope Gregory in 590 AD, is deadly sin. How can such a negative emotion be ascribed to God? Would it surprise you to learn that the Old Testament only applies this adjective to God and never to a human?

The Hebrew word that is translated into "jealous" is *qana*. Literally, the word means a strong emotion, which can be good or bad. An alternative translation for *qana* is *zealous*. There are many times in the Old Testament when *qana* gets translated as zealous instead: "The zeal of the LORD of hosts will do this" (2 Kings 19:31).

What exactly is a verse saying, then, when it uses *qana* for God? As a strong emotion, when applied to God, it is describing intense love, a love that is eager to protect what is precious to God. When God is called *qana*, his love is as a husband for a wife, a strong love that expects faithfulness, a love that is zealous to protect the relationship.

The Deuteronomy verse quoted above comes just before a listing of the commandments, which are familiar to us. Then following that, in the sixth chapter of Deuteronomy, we get the greatest commandment the Lord gave to his people. The Jewish people call it the *Shema*. The *Shema* is the central prayer, the prayer that Jewish children learn first. It is the text that is written out on parchment then rolled up and placed inside the *mezuzah* (a little container attached to the doorpost of a Jewish structure).

The *Shema* is the response to God's *qana*—the human equivalent, if you will:

> Hear, O Israel: The LORD is our God, the LORD alone. You shall love the LORD your God with all your heart and with all your soul, and with all your might. Keep these words that I am commanding you today in your heart. Recite them to your children and talk about them when you are at home and when you are away, when you lie down and when you rise. Bind them as a sign on your hand, fix them as an emblem on your forehead, and write them on the doorposts of your house and on your gates. (Deut 6:4–9)

If *qana* is God's declaration of love for his bride, then the *Shema* is the wedding vow of the bride for her husband. Thanks be to God!

Jehovah

God also said to Moses, "Thus you shall say to the Israelites, 'The LORD, the God of your ancestors, the God
of Abraham, the God of Isaac, and the God of Jacob,
has sent me to you': This is my name forever, And this
is my title for all generations." —Exod 3:15

This is a look at a word that is not found in the Bible. We think it
is, probably due to its frequency of use, such as the first line of the
great Welsh hymn, "Guide Me, O Thou Great Jehovah." In fact,
God's name is not actually Jehovah, and the word is not biblical.
Why, then, is it so commonly used?

When Moses encounters God at the burning bush in Exodus
3:13–15, during their conversation, Moses asks what God's name
is. He is told three rather puzzling titles, all of which relate to God's
existence, and none of which is a proper noun such as we might
recognize as a name.

Verse 14 gives *"Ehyeh-Asher-Ehyeh"* in Hebrew, translated
into English by three possibilities: "I am who I am," or "I am what
I am," or "I will be who I will be." Next, verse 14 gives *"Ehyeh,"* or
just "I am." Finally verse 15, offers *"YHWH,"* which will not actually be printed in the Bible. Jews avoided speaking this holy name,
and to avoid speaking it, they avoided writing it. As a substitu-
tion, they wrote the Hebrew word for *the Lord*, which is *Adonai*. In
English translations of the Bible, this will be shown as "the LORD",
with all capital letters.

That still does not reveal how the word *Jehovah* came to be
used. First, we must realize that, initially, Hebrew words printed
in the scripture did not include any vowels. These markings were
later added. Since *YHWH* is not pronounced, it was just assumed
that the missing vowels between the consonants should be the

same vowel sounds as heard in the word *Adonai*. Then, we must remember that before there were English translations of the Hebrew Bible, Latin translations were made. Since the Latin language does not have either a letter "Y" or a letter "W", substitutions had to be made for those letters, which resulted in "JHVH". Now it may be readily seen that when we add the vowel sounds of *Adonai* into the *tetragrammaton* (Greek word for "four letters"!), the result is *Jehovah*.

There are actually many different words and titles applied to God throughout the Bible. All are human attempts to use our own language and understanding to describe the Creator of the Universe. But I suspect God will hear us whichever title we do use. Thanks be to God!

Jubilee: Proclaim Release to the Captives

> The spirit of the Lord GOD is upon me, because the LORD has anointed me;
>
> he has sent me to bring good news to the oppressed, to bind up the brokenhearted,
>
> to proclaim liberty to the captives, and release to the prisoners; to proclaim the year of the LORD's favor.
> —Isa 61:1–2

What is this year of the Lord's favor that Isaiah mentions? To find out, we need to go back to the Torah, to the twenty-fifth chapter of Leviticus. Moses had been commanded by God that once the people were residing in Canaan, the "land shall observe a Sabbath for the LORD." Remember that observing a weekly Sabbath was a perpetual sign of the covenant for the people (Exod 31:12). For the land, a Sabbath meant six years of working the land and then one year of "complete rest for the land" (Lev 25:1–7).

That's not all! Every Hebrew indentured servant who had worked for six years was to receive manumission in the seventh year (Deut 15:12). Slaves, too, were to go free in the seventh year, after serving for six years (Exod 21:2). That's not even all! "Every seventh year you shall grant a remission of debts" (Deut 15:1). Isn't that something!

In the gospel of Luke, when Jesus begins his ministry, the first thing he does is go into the synagogue in Nazareth, where he was handed the scroll of Isaiah to read. It was open to Isaiah 61:1–2, the text quoted above. Jesus then said, "Today this scripture has been fulfilled in your hearing" (Luke 4:21). How?

We know that Jesus' ministry consisted of forgiving people and healing people. He got into trouble with the Jewish leaders because he tended to do this on the Sabbath day. If Jesus' healings were only about physical health, they could have occurred on any day of the week. Jesus goes out of his way to heal on the Sabbath. Why?

The essence of the Sabbath as a day of "rest" also has connotations of "rest" from any sort of debt. Just as the concept of a sabbatical year included release from bondage and forgiveness of debts, Jesus is reclaiming the Sabbath day. He is releasing people from their bondage to sin.

The concept of the sabbatical year gets even better, according to Leviticus. Every seven sets of seven years, there would be a bonus. The fiftieth year was called the Jubilee year. The name comes from the Hebrew word *Yovel*. A *yovel* is literally a blast from the trumpet, called a *shofar*, which is made from a ram's horn, which is a *yobhel*.

The Jubilee year included all of the remissions of the sabbatical and more. All property was to be returned to the original owner or heir. The idea behind this is that the people could only ever be tenants. Land could not be sold forever, because land did not belong to anyone except the Lord! This is a strong reminder of just how much is from God.

> And you shall hallow the fiftieth year and you shall proclaim liberty throughout the land to all its inhabitants. It shall be a jubilee for you; you shall return, every one of you, to your property and every one of you to your family. (Leviticus 25:10)

On July 8, 1776, a famous bell rang to summon people to hear a reading of the Declaration of Independence. Inscribed upon the Liberty Bell are these words from Leviticus: "Proclaim LIBERTY throughout all the land unto all the inhabitants thereof" (Lev 25:10). Thanks be to God!

Judge: Decide (New Testament)

The four Gospels that open the New Testament all work toward the Passion narrative of the life of Jesus. Jesus' death on the cross is the main event, and it is through the lens of this that we need to view God's ultimate judgment. That lens is forgiveness. Even from the cross, Jesus does not get angry; Jesus does not get judgmental; Jesus just forgives and dies.

The Greek verb *krine* can be translated as either "judge" or "decide". Jesus uses the verb in John's eighth chapter, the story of the woman caught in adultery. Jesus says to her, "Neither do I condemn you" (John 8:11). In fact, John wrote the verb *krine*, so it should be translated "judge". Later in the same chapter, Jesus says, "You judge by human standards; I judge no one" (John 8:15). Same verb.

Earlier in John's gospel, we read,

> Indeed, God did not send the Son into the world to condemn the world, but in order that the world might be saved through him. Those who believe in him are not condemned; but those who do not believe are condemned already, because they have not believed in the name of the only Son of God. And this is the judgment, that the light has come into the world, and people loved darkness rather than light. (John 3:17–18)

Again, the verb is not "condemn" but *krine*, "decide" or "judge".

This is the crux of the definition. The light has come into the world. It is our decision (*krine)* to follow the light rather than the darkness. Jesus does not make that decision for us. Jesus does not condemn. Everything Jesus does is focused on his saving.

The *krine* is ours. We make the choice. We pass judgment upon ourselves by our response to Christ.

When does this judgment, this *krine,* occur? At this very moment: "Now is the judgment of the world" (John 12:31).

If someone has chosen darkness over light, does that speak of predestination? No, because the choice is always and forever ours. Spiritual life and death are not just a future choice. People choose every day in their response to Jesus' revelation and in their treatment of each other in love.

It has been said that heaven is populated only by forgiven sinners, and hell is populated only by forgiven sinners. The only difference between them is their own acceptance or rejection. No one is out who wasn't already in! Thanks be to God!

Judge: Deliver (Old Testament)

> May the LORD therefore be judge, and give sentence between me and you. May he see to it, and plead my cause, and vindicate me against you. —1 Sam 24:15

> Then the LORD raised up judges who delivered them out of the power of those who plundered them. —Judg 2:16

For English speakers, the word *judge* has one connotation; it only suggests a court-like or judiciary action. Usually one party hears a case between two other parties in conflict; the judge then judges which party is in the right and what is to be done about it.

That is certainly the case in Genesis 16:5: "Then Sarai said to Abram, 'May the wrong done to me be on you! I gave my slave-girl to your embrace, and when she saw that she had conceived, she looked on me with contempt. May the LORD judge between you and me!'" The Hebrew word that translates as "judge" here is *sapat.*

But *sapat* is rich with definitions. Not always is it used in a judicial sense. Other functions that can be called *sapat* include leadership roles of a political or a military nature. Sometimes it means any process whereby law and order are maintained.

In the verse above quoted from First Samuel, there is a twist. The word that is translated from *sapat* is not "judge", it is "vindicate"! *Sapat* can just as often describe deliverance from oppression or injustice as any other definition. That is the sense of *sapat* as it is found in the book of Judges. In fact, a better title for the sixth book of the Bible would be "Deliverers". The men and women we meet in this book do not sit in courtroom-like judgment upon anyone; rather, they deliver their people from injustice and oppression.

Check out some of the short stories within the book of Judges, and you will meet some vivid characters: the left-handed Ehud (chapter 3), the fearless ladies Deborah and Jael (chapter 4), young Gideon (chapter 6), and strong-man Samson (chapters 13 through 16). Each rose up when needed and delivered their people.

Maybe this alternative will give you something to ponder the next time you recite the Apostles' Creed. What would it mean if "judge" were changed to "deliver"? "He will come again to deliver the living and the dead." Thanks be to God!

Judgment Seat

> Why do you pass judgment on your brother or sister?
> . . . For we will all stand before the judgment seat of
> God. For as it is written: "As I live, says the Lord, ev-
> ery knee shall bow to me, and every tongue shall give
> praise to God." So then, each of us will be accountable
> to God. Let us therefore no longer pass judgment on
> one another. —Rom 14:10–13

It is always important to determine, when examining a Bible passage, its context. These verses about judgment are situated in a
chapter advocating tolerance for the differences one encounters
among those who are Gentile Christians compared to Jewish
Christians (perhaps issues such as kosher vs. non-kosher; fasting
vs. non-fasting; Sabbath vs. Sunday).

A more ominous part of the passage from Romans is the
allusion to God's "judgment seat". Many people are brought up
believing that there will be a Judgment Day that includes the as-
signment of each soul to either heaven or hell, and God will be
sitting on the judge's bench making that call. But is that what this
passage actually says? Not at all.

Paul is referring to a passage from Isaiah (45:21), where Isaiah is challenging the people of all the nations (Gentiles) to judge
(i.e., decide) for themselves whether or not idols have any power
to save anyone. Then Isaiah tells the people that there is only one
God, a God who declares: "Turn to me and be saved, all the ends
of the earth! For I am God, and there is no other" (Isa 45:22). All
the nations, all people, are invited to seek salvation in the worship
of the only true God.

The idea of a "judgment seat" goes back to Exodus. God gave instructions for the making of the Ark of the Covenant, including a "mercy seat of pure gold" protected by cherubim. That was to be the location from which God would meet with the people. (Exod 25:17–22).

In the Hebrew Bible, the word now translated as "mercy seat" is *kapporeth*, which comes from the verb *kaphar*, meaning "to cover". Literally, the verb means to cover up or "wipe out", as in "wipe clean of impurities"! Once a year, on the high holy day of Yom Kippur, the high priest would enter the innermost sanctum of the Tabernacle (or Temple) and splash sacrificial blood on the *kapporeth*, praying that this would atone for the sins of the people. (Lev 16)

This gives an entirely different picture of how the sins of the people will be handled—wiped out by the blood of a sacrifice. Sacrificial blood of the Lamb . . . the Lamb of God! Thanks be to God!

Justification

> But now, apart from law, the righteousness of God
> has been disclosed, and is attested by the law and the
> prophets, the righteousness of God through faith in
> Jesus Christ for all who believe. For there is no distinc-
> tion, since all have sinned and fall short of the glory
> of God; they are now justified by his grace as a gift,
> through the redemption that is in Christ Jesus, whom
> God put forth as a sacrifice of atonement by his blood.
> —Rom 3:21–25

These words were at the heart of the Reformation begun by Martin
Luther. Paul, in this letter to the Romans, is making pretty bold
statements. Do you hear Paul proclaiming that God is freely acquit-
ting all sinners? Do you believe, as Paul does, that all this took place
on the cross, and that Jesus' sacrificial death was the center stage for
this gift of grace? Martin Luther believed Paul.

The Greek word for *righteousness* (*dikaiosune*) is only used
for God; it is an attribute belonging to God alone. The Greek
word for *justified* (*dikaioumenoi*) is a passive verb applied to us.
Notice that they both have the same root in Greek. We cannot call
ourselves righteous, only God is that, but justification is something we are granted by a gracious God. It means we are brought
into a right relationship with God. Remember in typing class
(now called keyboarding), when the margins are justified, they
are brought into alignment on both sides. That's a great metaphor
for our justification applied by God.

"For we hold that a person is justified by faith apart from
works prescribed by the law" (Rom 3:28). The justification we receive is not dependent upon anything we can do or not do. It does

not operate by works; it is apart from the law, but it does operate by faith. All are justified, but whether we recognize or accept this gift is dependent upon our belief. Justification sounds like our word "justice", so we might think it means you get what you deserve. But, the good news of God's justification of absolutely everyone, the whole of humankind, is that we don't get what we deserve, we get this merciful gift of grace instead. Thanks be to God!

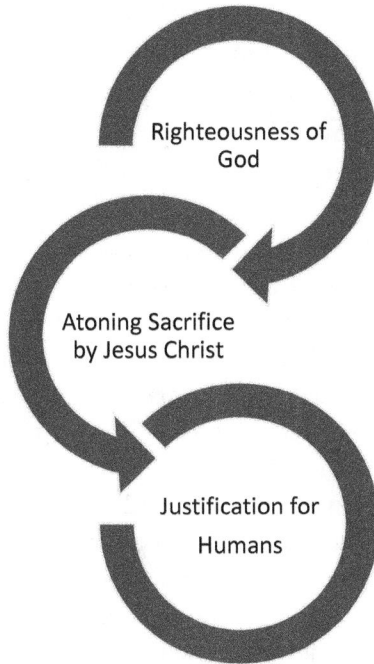

Righteousness of God

Atoning Sacrifice by Jesus Christ

Justification for Humans

Kenosis

> Let the same mind be in you that was in Christ Jesus,
> who, though he was in the form of God, did not regard
> equality with God as something to be exploited, but
> emptied himself, taking the form of a slave, being born
> in human likeness. And being found in human form,
> he humbled himself and became obedient to the point
> of death—even death on a cross. —Phil 2:5–8

The verb "emptied" in the verses above is from the Greek *ekenosen*, a verb form that means Christ "poured himself out". By emptying himself, it means the removal of any self-will. This enables a complete receptivity to God's divine will. The concept, in English, is called "kenosis". It can include the discarding of ones race, class, and gender in this self-emptying process. The idea is a stark contrast to the patronage system of the Roman Empire. That culture had definite class systems, with inequality and competition at every level. The apostle Paul envisioned instead a community that was "kenotic", based on cooperation and equality among everyone.

A secular example of kenosis is the clear difference in two current styles of educating children. The traditional, public school environment is based upon competition, rankings, tests, and grades. A Montessori approach offers, instead, an atmosphere of cooperation and sharing, with everything motivated by what is good for everyone. That is a kenosis.

We so easily overlook common words that are heard as regularly as "empty" or "emptied" are. By examining the original word of a text, with its various definitions, we have an opportunity to consider anew the extent or depth a word might carry with it. In this case, we are offered a lens to view the phrase "emptied himself" that allows us to pause and ponder. What we are shown in this case is the extent and depth of the love, the gift, we have been handed by Christ. Thanks be to God!

Koinonia

> I thank my God every time I remember you, constantly praying with joy in every one of my prayers for all of you, because of your sharing in the gospel from the first day until now.
>
> ... It is right for me to think this way about all of you, because you hold me in your heart, for all of you share in God's grace. —Phil 1:3–5, 7

An idea that we read twice in the passage above is "share/sharing", which is translated from the Greek *koinonia*, coming directly into English as koinonia. It describes more than just offering a portion of what you might have to another. It speaks to a full fellowship or communion with others, a joint participation that includes sharing anything with your community.

There are many words that are used to describe the sacrament of Holy Eucharist, the Lord's Supper, in which we participate in taking bread and wine, as instructed by our Lord Jesus at his Last Supper, when he offered these elements to the disciples as his own body and the new covenant in his blood. For those who call this sacrament Holy Communion, the word communion is also from koinonia! A sharing, indeed!

Whatever phrase your denomination uses for this special sacramental meal, the underlying intent is the gift of koinonia, a communal sharing, which is another way to view a relationship. Perhaps one of the great gifts we find in the Bible is that we have a God of relationship. Thanks be to God!

Law or Gospel

> Now we know that whatever the law says, it speaks to those who are under the law, so that every mouth may be silenced, and the whole world may be held accountable to God. —Rom 3:19

> "But now, apart from the law, the righteousness of God has been disclosed. —Rom 3:21

In his New Testament letters, Paul spends a lot of time writing about the concepts of law and gospel. What comes to mind for you, when you consider these two words? For many, the word law has connotations from myriad television offerings (*Dragnet, Perry Mason, Columbo, Law & Order, NYPD Blue*, to name a few). Or, perhaps, you think of idioms pervasive in our culture: "laying down the law", "in the eyes of the law", "law of the jungle", or "long arm of the law". Do you think immediately of the Ten Commandments? All of these are natural assumptions.

Then, what about gospel? Is it the first four books of the New Testament? Is it the good news of Jesus Christ, as evangelist Mark proclaims? Or, maybe, you see law vs. gospel envisioned as the Old Testament vs. the New Testament. Do you think the stern God of the Old Testament has been superseded by Gentle Jesus in the New?

When Paul writes the word "law", the Greek word used is *nomos*. The definitions for *nomos* include "law" or "principle". As you read a letter from Paul, you might be hearing him say "law", or he might be using a word-play, intending "principle".

In general, Paul is referring to the Torah, which is the first five books of the Old Testament. Literally, Torah means "the Teachings". The Torah, in Jewish understanding, was a great gift from God, a gift for an orderly existence as the people of God. The Teachings showed a way to live in harmony with one another, while being set apart as God's own.

Underlying this use of the term, Paul also wants his audience to realize the foundational principle of the Torah: "I am the LORD, your God; you shall have no other gods before me" (Exod 20:2). All else is a sub-set of that over-arching principle!

The Torah had not been given as a way to get righteousness. Indeed, in the Old Testament, only God is termed righteous, not human beings.

We cannot call ourselves righteous, only God is that, but through gospel grace, we can be in a right relationship with God. This does not negate the law, which is still a great gift of how to be identified as one of God's own. This right relationship is called justification by Paul. Interestingly, both "righteous" and "justified" are from the same Greek word. One is in noun form (God alone) and the other in verb form (what God does for us). Thanks be to God!

Jesus Christ Fulfills the Law in the Gospel

Law or Torah

Oh, how I love your law! It is my meditation all day long.
—Ps 119:97

If you ever had to (or tried to) memorize the list of all the books of the Bible, years later, even if out of practice, perhaps you can still manage to recite the first five books: Genesis, Exodus, Leviticus, Numbers, Deuteronomy. The Jewish tradition calls these five books *Torah*.

Generally, Torah, is understood as "Law", but the laws and legal codes are just one portion of the entire Torah. Literally, the word means "the teachings" or "instruction", and it is a derivative of the Hebrew verb that means "to shoot an arrow".

Although the Torah is a compilation of many traditions and sources and is not the work of one author, it is sometimes also called *torat moshe*, that is "instruction of Moses". Moses was not the author, but his authority is dominant. Apart from the narratives in Genesis, Moses is a main character in the rest of the Torah.

You may also hear these books grouped under the term *Pentateuch*. This is the Greek word for "five scrolls" (*pente* = five + *teuchos* = vessel). Essentially, the five books are only one book. Since the original written format would have been a scroll, the length would have been too long to be anything but cumbersome. Therefore, for the sake of convenience, it was divided into five separate scrolls.

For Jews, the Torah is the most holy book, above all the other books of the Hebrew Bible. It is believed that by studying and practicing Torah one renews intimacy with God. The Torah is the antidote to the evil inclination of humanity, a pathway toward eternal life.

It is also considered the foundational story for the Jewish people. The fact that stories predominate means that it is a very effective teaching tool. Thanks be to God!

> Hear, my child, your father's instruction [i.e., torah],
>
> and do not reject your mother's teaching [i.e., torah];
>
> for they are a fair garland for your head,
>
> and pendants for your neck. (Prov 1:8–9)

Lost

For the Son of Man came to seek out and save the lost.
—Luke 19:10

Your first bedtime stories were quite likely nursery rhymes, so you surely know the fate of Little Bo Peep's sheep; the sheep did not stay lost. And, they all lived happily ever after. Your first Sunday School stories probably included a Good Shepherd searching for one lost sheep until it was found. And, they all lived happily ever after.

That story of the Good Shepherd is actually found four chapters earlier in Luke than our verse above. Indeed, the fifteenth chapter of Luke has a trilogy of examples of lost items being found: a sheep in Luke 15:4, a coin in Luke 15:8, and a son in Luke 15:32. When we read about something being described as lost, we do so with the expectation of a reversal of that state. We readily pair lost with found. Lost at sea? Lost in space? Don't despair; just stay tuned until the season finale for a rescue.

The Greek word that is used throughout the four Gospels for lost is identical to the one in the verse above: *apololos*. Translating *apololos* as lost is entirely accurate, although it does tend to be euphemistic to our ears. We are so accustomed to pairing lost and found, that we do not as regularly recall the terminal tendency of lostness!

Interestingly, the root verb in Greek, *apollumi*, is absolutely fatalistic. Its definitions include to kill, to ruin, to destroy utterly, to make void, to perish, to die. There is no hint of just wandering away or straying off, to be rescued later. It's over. This is the end.

When Jesus refers to the house of Israel (Matt 15:24) . . . and by extension to us . . . as lost, think of it as "dead in their (our) tracks", and there is nothing we can do about it.

Wait, though! Luke's verse pairs our loss not with being found but with being saved. That's the plan. Lost and saved!

Here's the good news . . . actually the greatest news . . . from Jesus as found in John 18:9: "I did not lose a single one of those whom you gave me." Not only is this not the end for us, it is a much better conclusion. And, they all lived happily ever after. Thanks be to God!

Lovingkindness/Steadfast Love

> In your steadfast love you led the people whom you
> redeemed; you guided them by your strength to your
> holy abode. —Exod 15:13

> The LORD, the LORD, a God merciful and gracious,
> slow to anger, and abounding in steadfast love and
> faithfulness, keeping steadfast love for the thousandth
> generation, forgiving iniquity and transgression and sin.
> —Exod 34:6–7

> Be mindful of your mercy, O LORD, and of your
> steadfast love, for they have been from of old. Do not
> remember the sins of my youth or my transgressions;
> according to your steadfast love remember me, for
> your goodness' sake, O LORD! —Ps 25:6–7

Translating some original words from the Bible into English can be
rather difficult, because sometimes precise equivalents just do not
exist. One word in particular that has caused concern is the Hebrew
word *hesed*. In our verse above, it was translated as "steadfast love".
As this phrase, you will encounter it multiple times in the Old Testament, especially in the Psalms. The fullest meaning of the word,
however, just cannot be conveyed in English. Various English ver-
sions of the Bible have rendered it as "mercy", "loyalty", "goodness",
"favor" and "loving-kindness", which is a popular choice that was
coined by Bible translator Miles Coverdale in 1535.

    Hesed is not "kindness" in general, and it is not used to
describe kindness of any type between humans. It is always
used to describe God, with the intention of putting forth God's

steadfastness and persistence in his love for his covenant-people. *Hesed* is the loving-kindness of God that will not let Israel go, despite Israel's continual waywardness. For this reason, it is associated with God's covenant.

We know that God's determination toward the covenant results in God's need to exercise mercy again and again. For this reason, when the Old Testament was translated into Greek in the third century BC, the word *eleos* (mercy, pity) was chosen, and the Latin translation done by Jerome in the fourth century AD used the word *misericordia* (merciful) for *hesed*. The English choice of "steadfast love" comes somewhat closer to the fuller meaning, which is ideally a composite of love with strength and fidelity.

Actually, the English word that is closest to this *hesed* that God gives is "grace". We think of grace as a New Testament word, since that is where we will read it. The Greek is *charis*. Martin Luther, in his 1534 German translation of the Bible, realized that *hesed* is the equal of *charis*, and he translated both into the German *gnade,* that is *grace* in English.

God's steadfast love, *hesed*, is not a sentimental love, it is a love that abounds in all of the concepts listed above to a degree that is beyond our comprehension or ability to explain. It is undeserved on our part and forever sure on God's. Thanks be to God!

Magnificat/Songs of Deliverance

Hannah prayed and said, my heart exults in the LORD;

My strength is exalted in my God.

... There is no Holy One like the LORD, No one besides you;

There is no Rock like our God.

... The bows of the mighty are broken, but the feeble gird on strength.

... The LORD makes the poor and makes rich; He brings low, he also exalts.

... For the pillars of the earth are the LORD's,

And on them he has set the world.
—1 Sam 2:1–2, 4, 7–8

The book of Psalms, found near the center of the Bible, is the songbook of the Hebrew people. Psalms were an important part of their worship liturgy. But there are other songs included throughout the Bible; these are called *canticles*. A small, but important, genre amidst the canticles are the songs of deliverance, such as that excerpted above.

This canticle, a *Magnificat*, is sung by Hannah to rejoice in her being granted a child. Note the themes that pervade this song: lifting up the lowly, bringing down the mighty, and praising God for his faithful strength. If this sounds familiar, you will certainly recognize the lyrics of this next canticle: "My soul magnifies the Lord, and my spirit rejoices in God my Savior, for he has looked with favor on the lowliness of his servant. Surely, from now on all generations will call me blessed." This is the opening of the *Magnificat* sung by Mary, at the news she will be the mother of the Son of God. It is found in Luke 1:46–55. Mary's canticle repeats the expected themes of Hannah's canticle: "He has brought down the powerful from their thrones, and lifted up the lowly" (Luke 1:52).

The canticle of Mary is sung regularly in the vespers or evening prayer services of the Lutheran and Episcopal churches, and it is an option in the matins or morning prayer liturgies. There is evidence in 1 Samuel 18:6–7 that the regular role of women was to sing during any victory celebrations, so these songs of deliverance are typical.

Scholars think that the very oldest portion of our Bible is the song of deliverance found in Judges 5. This is attributed to Deborah, one of the important leaders during the time of the Judges. With similar themes of bringing down the mighty and lifting up the lowly, this canticle tells of the bravery of the woman Jael, who single-handedly won a victory against the enemy of the people.

The first canticle in the chronology of the Bible is found in the fifteenth chapter of Exodus. God has just separated the sea, and the Israelites, departing from Egyptian bondage, cross on dry land, but the pursuing Egyptian chariots will be lost as the sea closes back upon them. Verse 1 suggests Moses led the song, but that is an editorial addition! In truth, we learn in the twenty-first verse who led the song: "And Miriam sang to them: 'Sing to the LORD, for he has triumphed gloriously; horse and rider, he has thrown into the sea.'" In the verses printed below, you will recognize the themes mentioned.

The ancients imagined that music echoed through the celestial spheres. As you read through the lyrics of Miriam's "Song of the Sea", you can almost hear an angelic choir joining in:

> Who is like you, O LORD, among the gods?
>
> Who is like you, majestic in holiness, awesome in splendor, doing wonders?
>
> . . . In your steadfast love you led the people whom you redeemed;

you guided them by your strength to your holy abode.

. . . The LORD will reign forever and ever. (Exod 15:11, 13, 18)

Anyone who has ever heard Handel's *Messiah* and has been drawn irresistibly to join in the "Hallelujah Chorus" knows how songs can stir the hearts of humanity. Jewish tradition claims that Miriam's canticle is the first time God received a song of praise . . . and he liked it! Thanks be to God!

Hear, O kings; give ear, O princes; to the LORD I will sing, I will make melody to the LORD, the God of Israel. (Judg 5:3)

Manna

> The whole congregation of the Israelites complained
> against Moses and Aaron in the wilderness. The Isra-
> elites said to them, "If only we had died by the hand
> of the LORD in the land of Egypt, when we sat by the
> fleshpots and ate our fill of bread; for you have brought
> us out into this wilderness to kill this whole assembly
> with hunger." Then the LORD said to Moses, "I am go-
> ing to rain bread from heaven for you, and each day
> the people shall go out and gather enough for that day."
>
> . . . in the morning there was a layer of dew around
> the camp. When the layer of dew lifted, there on the sur-
> face of the wilderness was a fine flaky substance, as fine
> as frost on the ground. When the Israelites saw it, they
> said to one another, "What is it?" For they did not know
> what it was. Moses said to them, "It is the bread that the
> LORD has given you to eat." —Exod 16:2–4, 13–15

In this passage in Exodus and later in the eleventh chapter of
Numbers, we learn quite a bit about this strange "bread from
heaven". It was on the ground when the dew lifted in the morn-
ings, it was as flaky as frost, it would melt in the sun, and it did
not keep until a second day . . . except on the eve of the Sabbath, when it would last an extra twenty-four hours, since none
would appear on the Sabbath! It was versatile to prepare; it could
be baked or boiled. It tasted pleasingly like honeyed wafers. It
sustained the people for forty years. Can you imagine eating the
same thing every day for forty years?

But here's the thing about *manna* (which, by the way, is the
Hebrew for "what is it?"). Everyone got the same amount. There

was no surplus; there was no lack. There was no greed. There was no hoarding. There was no hunger. There were no "haves" or "have nots". There were no class distinctions.

Quite the lesson in God's economics! From this daily miracle of "bread from heaven", the people had to learn to depend on God alone. They had to learn that every moment of their very existence depended upon God alone and his daily miracles.

It turns out, even today there is a cash product produced in the Sinai called tamarisk manna, made from the crystallized globules that tamarisk plant lice secrete each day. It tastes like honey, abounds in carbohydrates, and is used by the Bedouin as a sweetener. That's the problem with miracles; they are in the eye of the beholder.

You may be surprised to learn that the very familiar Lord's Prayer has a petition requesting manna. Yes, when we pray, "Give us this day our daily bread," we are not being redundant, saying "day" *and* "daily". In the original Greek, the adjective we read as "daily" could have been translated as "supernatural", in other words "bread from heaven"! Even better, check out John 6:31–35 for more about this "bread of life"! Thanks be to God!

Mercy

> What then are we to say? Is there injustice on God's part?
>
> . . . For he says to Moses, "I will have mercy on whom I have mercy,
>
> and I will have compassion on whom I have compassion." —Rom 9:14

This verse from Paul's letter to Rome even troubles some adults in our Bible Study group. They worry that somehow, for some reason, *they won't* receive God's mercy or compassion. Do you hear the words the same way?

When other people hear those words, they might think, "Good! Sinful folks do not deserve to receive mercy; they get what they deserve!"

When Paul wrote this letter to the Romans, he was quoting an Old Testament verse, which he does quite regularly. He had been using as an example the story of the hardening of Pharaoh's heart in the Exodus narrative. God said to Moses: "I will be gracious to whom I will be gracious, and will show mercy on whom I will show mercy" (Exod 33:19).

That hardened heart still troubles people, because then it sounds as if it was predestined, that Pharaoh had no free will. Could it be that perhaps God used the hardening of Pharaoh's heart to advance God's purpose in the Exodus story, but the hardening of that heart was not something God inflicted upon Pharaoh? God allowed Pharaoh to suffer the consequences of his stubborn rebellion, to allow that progression to run its course.

The Creator's way, God's theodicy, is totally unaccountable to us. That's probably because we are the accountants. We keep track. We know who's been naughty and who's been nice, right? To us, Romans 9:14 might sound as if God is showing favoritism, because we are used to keeping score. We keep track of who followed the rules and who didn't, in almost a kindergarten mentality: *He cut in front of me! She touched my things! She got a bigger cookie than me! That's not fair!* Sound familiar?

Perhaps a better approach to Paul's verse is to remember God is the parent saying, "*I am* the one who decides what is fair. I can give cookies to everyone, if I want to do so. So, come to the table and we'll all have cookies!"

Paul is writing in the context that the bulk of Israel had not responded favorably to the gospel message of Jesus as Messiah. Would it not be terrible, Paul wonders, if Gentiles accepted the New Covenant while the original people who had first received God's covenant are left out? Paul's message is a reminder that it is God's choice to be gracious and compassionate and merciful to people that we might think have been left out. It's not up to us. Thankfully, it's up to God, and grace abounds. Thanks be to God!

Messiah

In the Old Testament, the word which we would understand as messiah is the Hebrew *mashiach*, which means "anointed one". When the word appears in the New Testament, we are reading the English rendition of the Greek, *Christos*. Again, it translates into "the anointed one". Anointing was done for consecration, which was the means for setting one apart for a special job or function. The high priest would have been anointed (Lev 4:3). Kings would have been anointed (1 Sam 10:1; 1 Kings 1:39). Prophets, too, would be anointed (1 Kings 19:15–16).

Observant Jews recite the *Amidah* prayer three times a day, in which one of the petitions is for a Messiah to come. Historically, however, there have been differing hopes for what a Messiah would do exactly. One model will be a *political* messiah, who could bring God's liberation, relying on God's law. Another model would be a *prophetic* messiah, who would bring God's restoration, through proclaiming words of truth. There is also a *priestly* model, a messiah who could make atonement or reconciliation with God, especially through sacrifice.

One of the biggest storylines in the Old Testament is that of Exodus, with Moses as God's mediator. The people were in bondage, but God, through Moses' political leadership, liberates them from slavery to Sabbath. The second biggest storyline is that of Exile, with all the prophets as God's mediators, speaking God's prophetic truth when people strayed from covenant. When the people are taken into exile, the ever-faithful God restores them to their homeland. Then there is the New Testament with the biggest storyline of all: the Good News of Jesus, Emmanuel, who offers the ultimate atonement for all to be reconciled with God.

There is an interesting account in the Gospels, in which the leader Moses, the prophet Elijah, and Jesus meet on a mountain-top; it is called the Transfiguration. It is as if the three biblical meta-narratives, of Exodus, of Exile, and of Expiation, intersect in a moment of time, just as the human and the divine coalesce in the incarnated Jesus. One might even say that "Ex-" marks the spot! Messiah might be an elusive word in the Old Testament, but the New Testament leaves no doubt as to our Messiah. Thanks be to God!

Original Sin

For I am ready to fall, and my pain is ever with me.

I confess my iniquity; I am sorry for my sin.
—Ps 38:17–18

We've all heard of "original sin", right? Could you name that sin? Wasn't it that apple incident in Genesis 3? Would you be surprised to know neither the word "apple" nor the word "sin" appears in that narrative?

The first mention of sin in our Bible is Genesis 4:7. The LORD says to Adam and Eve's firstborn, Cain, "If you do well, will you not be accepted? And if you do not do well, sin is lurking at the door; its desire is for you, but you must master it." You all know what happens next. The firstborn son, Cain, kills his brother, Abel.

Do you have a working definition of sin?

- Is it breaking one of the Commandments (i.e., defiance of God)? Don't forget that the first family lived long before these were given to Moses.

- Is it missing the mark? That's a literal definition taken from the vocabulary of archery.

- Is it a basic corrupting influence roaming in the universe? (The "devil" made me do it.)

- Is it something that separates us from God? Idolatry is our replacement of God as central by anything else.

Is it anything that is in opposition to God's benevolent purposes?

You may be familiar with the idea that, while we have only one word for "snow", the Eskimos have more than one word, because they distinguish among varying types of snow. Well, the Hebrew language had at least seven words that are translated as "sin". With varying definitions, such as "iniquity", "trespass", "offense", "wickedness", "transgression", "crime", "mischief", or "perversion" (*amal, asam, awen, awon, hatta't, pesa, rasa*), these words usually make it into the Bible as the one word: "sin". The one found in the Genesis 4:7 passage is *hatta't*, which literally means "to miss the mark".

The phrase "original sin" was coined by the early church father Irenaeus (in the second century AD) and developed by Augustine (in the fifth century AD). Their idea, based on letters by Paul, was that original sin is an inherited condition transmitted through procreation. It was Augustine who devised the terrifying concept that unbaptized infants who die go directly to hell! But none of that is biblical!

The Jewish tradition does not hold the first humans responsible for the sins of humanity. We can learn much about sin from the fourth chapter of Genesis, where it does originate. God describes it as a predatory animal. Have you ever felt that?

And, by Cain's question, whether sarcastic or ingenuous, we learn the heart of the matter: "Am I my brother's keeper?"

The fifty chapters of Genesis give us many examples of responses to that question in the stories of the patriarchs: brothers Cain and Abel; brothers Ishmael and Isaac; brothers Esau and Jacob; and, Joseph and his brothers. We wonder if the sibling rivalry will ever end!

When we read these narratives, we recognize themes that plague our world still. We may despair that there is no hope for mankind.

The book of Genesis, however, does ultimately give us the answer to Cain's question. In the last chapter of Genesis, we learn the correct response: Joseph *forgives* his brothers and *cares* for them. Yes, I am my brother's keeper. The last word is always forgiveness.

Happy are those whose transgression is forgiven, whose sin is covered.

Then I acknowledged my sin to you, and did not hide my iniquity;

I said, 'I will confess my transgressions to the LORD,'

and you forgave the guilt of my sin. (Ps 32:1, 5)

Thanks be to God!

Parousia or Second Coming (Advent)

These words seem to be used inter-changeably, but that is, in fact, quite problematic. First, you should know that the phrase "second coming" is just not found as such in the New Testament. The word we do find, a handful of times, especially in Matthew 24, is the word *parousia*. The Greek comes directly into English.

Like many Greek words, it is a "compound", made up of *para*, which is usually translated as "near" or "with", and *ousia*, which means "being" or "existing". Keep in mind that one of the things that gets Jesus in trouble with the Jewish authorities is his reference to himself using the designation of God, "*I am*" (*ego eimi*), which, to first-century Jewish listeners, would definitely recall the holy name God told Moses in the third chapter of Exodus. *Parousia* is a noun, describing a state of existence, and it is not a verb or participle suggesting a future action.

If we look at the same Matthew passage in Greek, we will notice that in addition to *parousia* being used a handful of times, the evangelist also uses the quite different word *erchomenon* in the same chapter; this is only translated as "coming". So, Matthew obviously is separating the verb he knows as "come" or "coming" from the word *parousia* he is also using. What did Matthew intend?

When translators wanted to render *parousia* into Latin, they combined the preposition *ad-* (which can mean at, to, towards, near, with, before, toward, about, until, at, on, by, about, almost—talk about multipurpose!) with the verb *venire* (which can be to come, to appear, to enter) to form *adventus*. Now we have a noun that is defined in Latin lexicons as an arrival, an approach, a visit, a visitation! Already or yet to come?

We learn from the Gospel of John that the Word made flesh has been here all along. So, why would *parousia* be understood as second coming instead of presence? If we think of *parousia* as a second coming, we are left with a timeline where Jesus just punctuates history instead of abiding always as a presence within history. Absence or presence? Which would you choose?

"For, lo, I am with you always, even to the end of the age" (Matt 28:20).

Thanks be to God!

Re-membrance

> Then he took a loaf of bread, and when he had given
> thanks, he broke it and gave it to them, saying, "This
> is my body, which is given for you. Do this in remem-
> brance of me." —Luke 22:19

These very familiar "words of institution" for the Lord's Supper (or
Holy Communion or Holy Eucharist) tell us Jesus desired "remem-
brance". What do you think when you hear this? Is this just an act
of recalling something that happened centuries ago? Could there be
anything more to it than just activation of a memory?

The Greek term for memory is *mneme*, a word that comes
directly into English, meaning a "memory unit". It is the root for
the English word mnemonic. Did Jesus wish to give us a reminder,
something to jog our memories with this verse?

Paul, in his first letter to the Corinthians, uses *anamnesin*
when he recounts the Lord's Supper (1 Cor 11:23–26). We see the
root word for memory in that word.

Consider the English again. "Remember" usually means
recall, bring to memory, or do not forget. However, it also can
mean to "re-member" or "re-animate" something by restoring it,
by putting the pieces back together again. Remarkably, in Paul's
next chapter of the letter, he explains that a body is composed of
many members (such as a foot or a hand, an eye or an ear), then
he continues this concept by explaining that the Body of Christ
is made up of individual living members, which are supposed to
be each of us.

So, yes, we must recall or remember this memorial meal
of bread and wine. More importantly, we take this sustenance
to reanimate, to reconstitute the very Body of Christ—as living
members. Whenever you take this sacrament, re-member what's

happening to you, to us, as the Body of Christ. Indeed, a resurrection of the Body!

Thanks be to God!

Redeemer

They remembered that God was their rock, the Most
High God their redeemer. —Psalm 78:35

I know that my Redeemer lives. —Job 19:25

Some of us might recognize this verse from Job as the opening
lyrics of a Christian hymn found in most church hymnals and
frequently sung at Easter. Even more folks would identify this as
one of the pieces in the famous oratorio written in 1741 by George
Frideric Handel: *Messiah*. In both instances the "Redeemer" refers
undoubtedly to Jesus Christ.

There are a couple of surprising things about the title "Redeemer". First, it is not found even once in the entire New Testament. Second, it is found in the Old Testament but never referring
to Jesus Christ. The Hebrew word that is translated into redeemer is
go'el. But sometimes *go'el* is translated as "kinsman" or "next-of-kin",
which is the case in the beautiful book of Ruth in the Old Testament.
The short story tells the tale of Ruth, a widow, who asks a near relative of her deceased husband to act as *go'el*, which will involve mar-
rying her. Naturally the man, Boaz, agrees, and the couple becomes
the great-grandparents for future King David.

In the complex legal codes of Leviticus, Numbers, and Deuteronomy, the duties of a *go'el* are addressed, in cases involving
relatives experiencing serfdom, slavery, widowhood, injury, or
death. The *go'el* is the nearest of kin who is to take the responsibil-
ity of vindicating the helpless relative.

The reassuring nature of *go'el* shines forth in its usage
throughout Isaiah. The great prophet casts God as the redeemer
for his people:

Thus says the LORD, the King of Israel,

and his Redeemer, the LORD of hosts: I am the first and
I am the last;

besides me there is no god. (Isa 44:6)

So, when we read in the various Isaiah passages about God as
the Redeemer, we must apply the Hebrew definition for the word
goʾel. That, of course, is the next-of-kin. Isaiah reassures his listeners that God, the Redeemer of Israel, will redeem the people from
their captivity. God is identifying himself as our closest relative.
What could be more reassuring! God is our nearest relative, who
accepts the role of *goʾel* for us, the one who accepts the duty of
righting the wrongs and restoring us. Thanks be to God!

Remnant

And Isaiah cries out concerning Israel, "Though the number of the children of Israel were like the sand of the sea, only a remnant of them will be saved." —Rom 9:27

So too at the present time there is a remnant, chosen by grace. —Rom 11:5

Paul was entirely familiar with the Hebrew scriptures and regularly drew upon them to support his epistles. In Romans we find nearly seventy quotes, including twenty from Isaiah. One of the themes that pervades Isaiah (as well as other prophets), which Paul applied in his letter to the Romans, is that of a *remnant*. The remnant can be a group of people who survive a catastrophe, or it could be a minority of people who are faithful amidst others who might not be. God's purpose for the remnant, in any case, is to assure his promise will be carried forward. The future of the "part" gives the future to the "whole".

An early example of a remnant is Noah, who was saved with his family on an ark filled with pairs of animals. For the Old Testament prophets, from Jeremiah to Micah, the remnant was the representative people who would return to Jerusalem from Babylonian exile in order to rebuild. The prophets spoke of God's promises of restoration and reconciliation after the humiliating exile.

For Paul, the remnant ideology applies to the problem of non-believing Jews, the bulk of the Jewish population who did not accept Jesus as the Christ, the Messiah. Paul was Jewish, of course, and he loved his kinfolk. He knew God's blessings and promises to them remain irrevocable. So, how can he reconcile the tremendous problem that they do not recognize his Messiah?

You may be one of thousands of people who have sent a DNA sample to ancestry.com, in order to find out more about your family tree. Paul also wrote about a family tree—the tree of God's "People of the Promise". Paul's explanation in Romans 11:17–24 involves an allegory of olive-grafting. The olive tree in God's garden is the people of God, the orchard farmer. The tree grows from the mature roots of the patriarchs. Some of the branches are believing Israelites, but other living branches are Gentiles who've been grafted onto the tree. Non-believing Israelites may have fallen from the tree, but here's the good news about Paul's orchard farmer. The living tree, the grafted branches, and the pruned limbs are all utterly dependent upon God's grace for their future. Those fallen branches may be grafted back onto the living tree at any time . . . in God's time. Thanks be to God!

Sabbath

> So God blessed the seventh day and hallowed it, because on it God rested from all the work that he had done in creation. —Gen 2:3

> Remember the sabbath day, and keep it holy. For six days you shall labor and do all your work. But the seventh day is a sabbath to the LORD your God; you shall not do any work—you, your son or your daughter, your male or female slave, your livestock, or the alien resident in your towns. For in six days the LORD made heaven and earth, the sea, and all that is in them, but rested the seventh day; therefore the Lord blessed the sabbath day and consecrated it. —Exod 20:8–11

Most folks believe that the first time we find the word "Sabbath" in the Bible is in the story of creation in Genesis. But check out the first verse quoted above . . . and you will not see it. Not in English, that is. Rest assured, however, it does appear in the Hebrew Bible. The word is *Shabbat*. In English, we read the word "rested", but the actual intention in the passage is that this is a cessation rather than a rest-period. God ceased working because creation was accomplished, not because he was tired.

The commandment shown from the Exodus passage quoted above is actually the longest commandment of the *Decalogue*. We know that observance of the Sabbath was a cornerstone of the Israelite religious practice from the earliest times, an observance well regulated by the Levite tribe of priests. For people who had been slaves for centuries in Egypt and later in Babylonia, the idea of a day each week of resting from their labors was a unique and liberating gift from God. Yes, rest from work is important, but is that the most important idea behind the Sabbath?

Whenever the people ceased from work, they ceased from worldliness. This was a way to keep holy! It was a regular, recurring reminder that they belonged to God, as they were separated from the rest of the world. This marked them as holy people.

When the people were in exile in Babylonia, they no longer had the Temple as central in their midst. With the Temple demolished, they had to ask themselves, "Where do we find God *now*?" They formerly had believed God dwelt inside the Temple . . . within the Holy of Holies, that most sacred space. Observing the Sabbath taught them that God is not relegated to a particular space. God can also be found in time, a holy time set aside each week.

When we read the story of the covenant between God and Israel, as expressed in the story in Exodus, we learn that even though circumcision was a sign of the covenant between God and Abraham and his male descendants, there is now a new sign of the covenant between God and the people.

> The LORD said to Moses: "You yourself are to speak to the Israelites; 'You shall keep my Sabbaths, for this is a sign between me and you throughout your generations, given in order that you may know that I, the LORD, sanctify you. You shall keep the Sabbath because it is holy for you. . . . Therefore the Israelites shall keep the Sabbath, observing the Sabbath throughout their generations, as a perpetual covenant. It is a sign forever between me and the people of Israel.'" (Exod 31:12–14, 16–17)

So, the Sabbath is much more than just a day off from work! It is meant to be a day off, or time off, from worldliness and given over to holiness. Thanks be to God!

Salvation

For in hope we were saved. —Rom 8:24

If you confess with your lips that Jesus is Lord and believe in your heart that God raised him from the dead, you will be saved. —Rom 10:9

For, everyone who calls on the name of the Lord shall be saved. —Rom 10:13

Have you ever been confronted in a public place by an individual you do not know, who approaches you and others around, asking, "Have you been saved?" Do you respond? Paul gives us some possible, even succinct, responses in the letter to the Romans.

When the evangelist Matthew uses the same Greek word, an equally plausible translation is "deliver/delivered" (Matt 1:21; 8:25; 14:30; 16:25; 27:40). The Greek word has the intention of asking for deliverance from despair and delivering renewed life with its possibilities and opportunities. It can mean prevent us from perishing right now.

In Romans 10:9, Paul seems to be equating "saved" with "justified", another equally acceptable understanding. There is a deeper meaning for Paul. His tenth chapter draws deeply from Deuteronomy 30, and he may have expected that his Roman audience would hear the connection. In Deuteronomy, Moses had prophesied the path that Israel would follow. He foresaw they would enjoy the covenant blessings, they would fall away from adherence to the covenant, most notably resulting in Babylonian Exile, but they would ultimately experience God's mercy upon their restoration to the promised land. Paul sees a parallel to this in the people's belief, or unbelief in the Messiah. The coming of the Messiah signaled the final stage of restoration and renewal of the covenant promises. For Paul, all of scripture directs us to Christ.

So, the fascinating thing to examine in the verses above is that the tenses vary! In Romans 8:24, which is a quote from the Old Testament—Joel 2:32, the verb is in the aorist tense, which is not a tense even identified in English. It means that a single event happened in the past, i.e., "one and done". At other times Paul speaks of salvation in the present (1 Cor 1:18), and yet other times as a future event (1 Cor 3:15). For Paul, salvation is complex. A timeline would have to show salvation at every point along the line!

What we do know, from Paul's use of the full narrative of scripture is that God's purposes will be fully and finally realized for all creation. Thanks be to God!

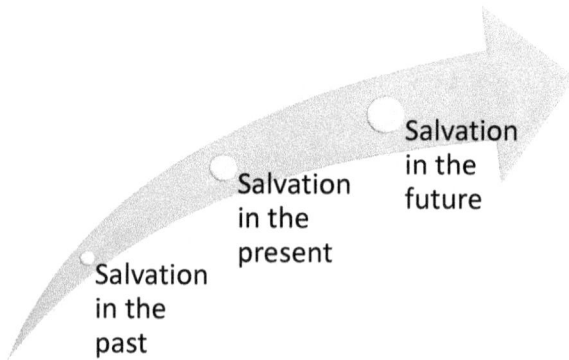

Salvation in the future

Salvation in the present

Salvation in the past

Sanctification

> But now that you have been freed from sin and en-
> slaved to God, the advantage you get is sanctification.
> The end is eternal life. —Rom 6:22

In the chapters of Romans leading up to this verse, Paul has presented every aspect of his thoughts on sin & law, law & grace, and
sin & grace. He then presents the conclusion that what Christ has
done, "once for all" is free us from sin. For many Christians, their
theology ends right there. What else could there be?

Well, Paul then inserts the next phase of the process, which
is the work of the Holy Spirit. Our creation (the work of the Father) is behind us; our redemption (the work of the Son) has been
accomplished (on Good Friday). Now, the Holy Spirit continues
to work without ceasing to sanctify us. The Greek verb *hagias-
mon*, with the root, *hagia*, translates unequivocally to the passive
verb, "to make holy", or sanctify.

Paul addresses the baptized in his letters as "saints", which is
hagios, or "holy ones". No church committee needed to determine
their qualifications for sainthood; it is a status he associated with
baptism. You, dear Christians, are saints!

What are some of the benefits of sanctification? It is the power to stand against sin. After you've been so decidedly lifted out of
sin's power, would it not be unthinkable to continue living under
the influence of sin? Sanctification is the power to transform your
life. It is the power to attain "maturity, to the measure of the full
stature of Christ" (Eph 4:13).

So, does this mean sanctification is only a New Testament
concept? By no means! Consider Ezekiel 36:22–27, in which God
cleanses the people through a sprinkling of clear water, then the

Lord gives them a new heart, and the Spirit of the Lord is put into human hearts! That's sanctification! Thanks be to God!

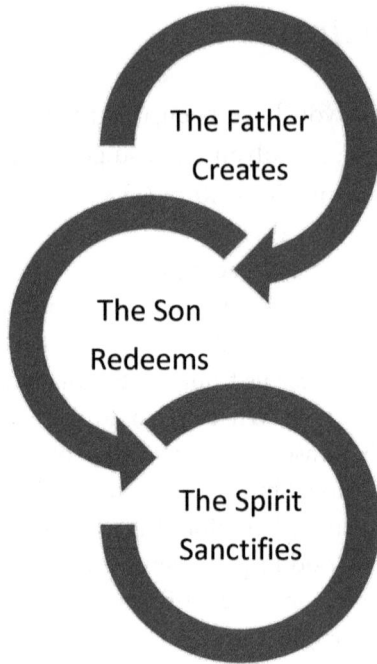

The Father Creates

The Son Redeems

The Spirit Sanctifies

(The) Satan

> One day the heavenly beings came to present them-
> selves before the LORD, and the Accuser also came
> among them to present himself before the LORD. The
> LORD said to the Accuser, "Where have you come
> from?" The Accuser answered the LORD, "From going
> to and fro on the earth, and from walking up and down
> on it." —Job 2:1-2

As you read this start to the familiar tale of Job, you may be
wondering whom this "Accuser" could be. Maybe you have read
a translation that substitutes the word "Satan" instead. Both Accuser and Satan are accurate for the text. In the Hebrew original,
the word was *"ha-satan"*, which translates as "the Accuser" or "the
Adversary". The definite article "the" is very much a part of the
translation. Satan is not the first name of any being to be found in
the Old Testament. Nor is the word "devil" used.

The book of Job is a very ancient story, and the plot begins
with the Lord speaking to one of the members of a divine council.
As explained in the story, this *ha-satan* is sort of an independent
prosecutor, who suggests that Job is only a blameless and upright
individual because God has blessed him so richly. The *ha-satan*
then undertakes to prove this to God.

Of the 23,145 verses in the Old Testament, apart from this
opening prologue in Job, *ha-satan* is used just two more times. One
of these is in the third chapter of the minor prophet Zechariah:

> Then he showed me the high priest Joshua standing be-
> fore the angel of the LORD, and the Adversary standing
> at his right hand to accuse him. And the LORD said to

the Adversary, "The LORD rebuke you, O Adversary!" (Zech 3:1–2)

Again, *ha-satan* is "the Adversary", acting very like a prosecuting attorney, or in popular terms, a "devil's advocate".

The point is that even though there is lots of sinning going on throughout the Old Testament, no one could ever say, "The devil made me do it." Nothing in 23,140 verses identifies a supernatural enemy of mankind named Satan who can wrench us from the embrace of God. Thanks be to God!

Serpent

> Now the serpent was more crafty than any other wild animal that the LORD God had made. He said to the woman, "Did God say, 'You shall not eat from any tree in the garden?'" —Gen 3:1

Using just the clues from the verse, and not your personal opinion, what do we learn about the serpent in the verse above? It was "crafty" ("shrewd" in the Hebrew Bible). It was a "wild animal" and not a supernatural creature. It had been made by God, right along with the rest of creation. It was living in the garden, with all of the animals and the humans, all of which, not much earlier, had been found to be "good" and had been blessed by God. It is never called "Satan" or "the devil". In Hebrew, not even the word "serpent" is used; in fact, the word is *nahash*, which means "one that bites."

Serpents do play a part in a curious story found in the book of Numbers:

> [The Israelites] set out by the way to the Sea of Reeds, to go around the land of Edom; but the people became impatient on the way. The people spoke against God and against Moses, "Why have you brought us up out of Egypt to die in the wilderness? For there is no food and no water, and we detest this miserable food." Then the LORD sent poisonous serpents among the people, and they bit the people, so that many Israelites died. The people came to Moses and said, "We have sinned against the LORD and against you; pray to the LORD to take away the serpents from us." So Moses prayed for the people. And the LORD said to Moses, "Make a poisonous serpent, and set it on a pole; and everyone who is bitten shall look at it and live." So Moses made a serpent of bronze, and put it upon a pole; and whenever

a serpent bit someone, that person would look at the serpent of bronze and live. (Num 21:4–9)

Although the serpents in this tale are called "poisonous, the Hebrew Bible has the word "fiery", and interestingly, the word for "fiery" or "burning" is *seraph*". That has led some to very mistakenly assume that the angels known as *seraphim* must be winged snakes!

Moses' bronze serpent-on-a-stick evidently travels throughout the wilderness sojourn with the Israelites, because it ends up in Solomon's Temple, where many years later, King Hezekiah decided some reforms were needed: "He broke in pieces the bronze serpent that Moses had made, for until those days the people of Israel had made offerings to it; it was called Nehushtan" (2 Kings 18:4). *Nehushtan* is "the one who bites".

What is the Numbers story teaching? Could it be as simple as telling the people to face their fears head-on instead of whining? In any event, beware of ones that bite! Thanks be to God!

Tabernacle

> Then the cloud covered the tent of meeting, and the glory of the LORD filled the tabernacle. Moses was not able to enter the tent of meeting because the cloud settled upon it, and the glory of the LORD filled the tabernacle. —Exod 40:34–35

> And the Word became flesh and lived among us, and we have seen his glory, the glory as of a father's only son, full of grace and truth. —John 1:14

These two verses appear to be decidedly disparate. In the passage from Exodus, you may recognize the word "tabernacle" as the portable tent that accompanied the Israelites during their forty years of sojourning in the wilderness, after the LORD led them out of bondage in Egypt.

Curiously, though, in this verse from John, the word that shows up in English as "lived" is actually translated from the Greek verb *eskenosen*, which is tabernacled, as a verb! An entirely different word would be used for the verb "lived".

Have you ever slept in a tent? Many of us have childhood memories of camping, either on family vacations or with Scouting troops. Pitching tents in new places allows us to enjoy the great outdoors in a variety of locations. What does a tent have to do with God?

Evangelist John intentionally wishes his audience to hearken back to the Old Testament traditions of God's presence among his people. In Hebrew, the word *Shekhinah* is translated as either "Glory" or the "Very Presence of God", and it refers to God's dwelling with the people. The tradition begins in Exodus 40:34, when the Presence of the LORD filled the tabernacle, which was the tent built according to the Lord's specific instructions. The *Shekhinah* would remain in the tabernacle with the people.

In the time of King David, the LORD told the prophet Nathan, "I have not lived in a house since the day I brought up the people of Israel from Egypt to this day, but I have been moving about in a tent and a tabernacle" (2 Sam 7:6). The LORD later moves the cloud of his Presence into the House of the LORD when Solomon built the Temple (1 Kings 8:10–13). The people got into the habit of thinking God was only in the tabernacle and later in the Temple.

During the period of the Babylonian exile, a great concern of the people was where the Presence of the LORD would be, since the Temple had been destroyed. The prophet Ezekiel was shown, in technicolor visions, the Glory of the Lord departing from the doomed Temple. Ezekiel's final vision gives witness to the return of the Glory, which was larger than the perfected Temple could even accommodate.

The theme of the Lord's presence among the people, encamping with them, is what evangelist John refers to in his prologue. God will be among us wherever we may pitch our tents, and the image of a portable tent, a tabernacle, emphasizes our God is not a stationary God. Thanks be to God!

Theophany

Who shall ascend the hill of the LORD? And who shall
stand in his holy place? —Ps 24:3

It is remarkable how many men in Bible stories encounter God
when they've ascended a mountain. An encounter or experience of
the divine, like we read about in the Bible, is called a *theophany*,
based on the Greek word for God, which is *theos*. We could name
Abraham, who had a theophany atop Mt. Moriah (Gen 22), where
he had gone to sacrifice his beloved son, at God's command. Jewish
tradition is that Mt. Moriah is the exact location where the Temple
was built centuries later, where God's own beloved Son will reveal
himself! These were truly mountain-top experiences!

Moses had his theophanies atop Mt. Sinai, both in the burning bush incident (Exod 3) and when he received the commandments (Exod 20). Moses' brother Aaron met his death . . . and God
. . . atop Mt. Hor (Num 20); Moses himself met God for the last
time on Mt. Nebo (Deut 34) at his own death, when God himself
buried Moses.

The entire Israelite company, thousands who had just es-
caped from bondage to slavery in Egypt, had a group theophany
of epic proportions at Mt. Sinai, just before learning of the commandments which God was to give them. There were atmo-
spheric manifestations that were terrifying which accompanied
the voice of God.

Elijah experienced the divine atop Mt. Carmel (1 Kings 18).
Even Jesus climbed mountains to be nearer God—check out Luke
9:28-36 and Luke 22:39. Is the Bible teaching us something about
pinnacles, or are they just metaphoric? It is interesting how often
the Bible stories place men on mountaintops for theophanies.

What about women? You may be surprised, but there is also a geographical location that seems to reflect the feminine! In Genesis 16, Hagar, mother to Ishmael, becomes the first character in the Bible to see an angel, who then shows her a well. Although not theophanies, Isaac's wife, Rebekah, is met at a well, Jacob will meet his wife, Rachel, at a well, and Moses meets his wife, Zipporah, at a well! As the source for water, wells are symbolic of life itself. The very longest recorded conversation with Jesus takes place with a woman at a well (*John 4*). Technically, that conversation would have been a theophany!

Keep alert for a theophany, wherever you are! Thanks be to God!

Toledoth

> Abraham took another wife, whose name was Keturah. She bore him Zimran, Jokshan, Medan, Midian, Ishbak, and Shuah. Jokshan was the father of Sheba and Dedan. The sons of Dedan were Asshurim, Letushim, and Leummim. The sons of Midian were Ephah, Epher, Hanock, Abida, and Eldaah. —Gen 25:1–4

Everyone dreads reading aloud the long listings of names of all the ancestors in the Bible. The boring listing of unpronounceable names: Mehujael . . . Mahalalel . . . Arpachshad . . . *really?* These are the Words of Life?

In the book of Genesis alone, we find ten such genealogies. Certainly, they are included as a literary bridge between generations in the narrative. The Hebrew word for these is *toledoth*. Our Bible is regularly punctuated by toledoth.

Apart from the difficult names, you may notice that there are impossibly long lifespans recorded, especially in Genesis:

> When Adam had lived one hundred thirty years, he became the father of a son in his likeness, according to his image, and named him Seth. The days of Adam after he became the father of Seth were eight hundred years; and he had other sons and daughters. Thus all the days that Adam lived were nine hundred thirty years; and he died. (Gen 5:3–4)

Many of these ages are such large numbers that we ask ourselves if people really lived that long. But these ages do not represent longevity, instead they suggest the greatness or goodness of the person: the older, the greater. Other near eastern literature also gives exaggerated ages. An ancient Mesopotamian text listing

Sumerian kings reports life spans in the thousands. Realistic age spans are suggested in Psalm 90:10: "The days of our lives are seventy years, or perhaps eighty, if we are strong."

Most ancient cultures viewed life as cyclical, just like the seasons of the year. The lives of individuals were not of value. If entire populations were wiped out, others would take their place. All that mattered was that there would be farmers or soldiers to serve a king.

But the Hebrew people had a different perspective. *Toledoth* was more than just keeping bloodlines or tribal affiliations orderly. *Toledoth* supported the concept that, being made in the image of God, every individual was *valued* by God. Being remembered by God *was* life.

So, as we read these challenging lists, do not be tempted to skip them. Every name is an individual valued by God. This is the Word of the Lord. Thanks be to God!

Tree of Life

> Then the angel showed me the river of the water of
> life, bright as crystal, flowing from the throne of God
> and of the Lamb through the middle of the street of
> the city. On either side of the river is the tree of life
> with its twelve kinds of fruit, producing its fruit each
> month; and the leaves of the tree are for the healing of
> the nations. —Rev 22:1–2

Art from several ancient cultures depicts the tree of life symbol.
Trees are actually symbolic in the Bible, also.

The book of Ezekiel uses trees full of life as allegories in chapters 17 and 31; then in Ezekiel 47:12, we read of trees with "leaves
for healing", as the prophet describes his final vision for God's restoration of the Temple, within a city to be named "The LORD is
There" (Ezek 48:35).

Our verse above is from the conclusion of the New Testament. Our Bible ends with a very special tree.

The Greek word for tree, *dendron*, is found in the four gospels
and in Revelation 9:4. Oddly, however, the verse quoted above,
Revelation 22:2, does not use the same Greek word. The unique
"tree of life" in the last chapter of the Bible uses a totally different
word, *xylon*, which is more accurately translated as lumber. Is that
important? John of Patmos clearly knew the difference between
the two words, since he's used them both. What he wants his audience to hear is the difference between those two words—a difference that in English would be like saying "timber" versus "lumber".
One is standing, and one is cut!

The other place we find *xylon* in the Bible is in Acts of the
Apostles (Acts 5:30; 10:39; 13:29). In each of those instances,

evangelist Luke is describing the death of Jesus by "hanging him on a tree". There is no question that the tree is the cross.

John's final image of the tree of life, indeed, our final encounter with a tree in the full scope of the biblical narrative, is not a restoration of one of the trees in the garden of Eden. Rather, this tree, which brings healing and redemption, is central to the revisioning, literally a revelation of the new city where God will dwell with his creatures. This tree is the *real* tree of life . . . which is, the cross that leads to life. That's the crux of the story!

Thanks be to God!

Vengeance/Retribution

Beloved, never avenge yourselves . . . for it is written, "Vengeance is mine, I will repay, says the Lord." —Rom 12:19

The verse above is in the section of Romans in which Paul lists the standards for how they are to act. We might call the advice practical instruction for living as a Christian.

As straight-forward as it sounds, it will be helpful to understand the background for this verse about vengeance. Paul is directly quoting Deuteronomy 32:35, which sought to limit escalating revenge that might lead to blood feuds. This particular teaching is given a Latin term, *lex talionis,* which we might call "an eye for an eye" approach. But in the Old Testament, the concept of vengeance by God was better understood as vindication or justice rather than revenge.

Paul's word is the Greek *ekdikesis*, which is a compound word with "justice" at its root. God is the one who dispenses justice. Paul's word for repay, *antapodoso*, is another compound word, with the root based on "give". It can mean repay, but it can also mean release or pardon, recompense or reward! God will dispense this repayment or pardon, but the object or person to whom this is offered is not identified!

Knowing what we know about Jesus' messages about forgiveness, it is more than likely that the verse, both in the Old Testament and when quoted in the New, is suggesting that rather than thinking God will hurl thunderbolts and lightning upon the perpetrator of an injustice that instead God will offer recompense to the injured party. Something to think about! Thanks be to God!

Yoke

> Come to me, all you that are weary and are carrying heavy burdens, and I will give you rest. Take my yoke upon you, and learn from me, for I am gentle and humble in heart, and you will find rest for your souls. For my yoke is easy, and my burden is light. —Matt 11:28–30

It has not been two hundred years since citizens of our country engaged in practices of slavery. It is in connection with slavery that many of us pair the word yoke. The yoke of slavery was a blot on our collective conscience. If we were to be asked what a yoke is, the concept of inescapable slavery and servitude might be our basis for a reply. When Jesus suggests that we take his yoke, we might misinterpret that, knowing that his path will be one of carrying a cross to its ultimate destination.

It has been two thousand years since Jesus made this remark about taking up his yoke. The Greek word is *zylos*, which can be defined as crossbar, team, pair, yoke, or the balancing beam of a scale used for weight measurement. Of course, these words primarily stem from an agricultural use, which those of us, who are mostly removed from farm life these days, dwelling in suburbs and cities, just do not encounter regularly.

Nevertheless, those Greek definitions transfer perfectly to our language. The English definitions of yoke include a wooden crosspiece fashioned over the necks of two people, a pair of anything, the shoulder piece for carrying a brace of buckets, a bond or union, as in marriage, or servitude.

Interestingly, all these variations involve some sort of connection. A yoke is not primarily defined as an implement for forcing one to perform hard work; it is predominantly a method of sharing a work load. If someone is yoked to you, it makes your job only half as difficult, since you will be joined with someone pulling with you.

Do not picture the yoke itself as the burden, rather imagine a strong partner on your side, sharing all the heavy lifting. Whatever you might have as a burden, it will not be borne alone, if one is joined in a yoke with another.

Thanks be to God!

Concluding Benediction

"The LORD bless you and keep you;
The LORD make his face to shine upon you,
And be gracious to you;
The LORD lift up his countenance upon you,
And give you peace."
(Num 6:24–26)

Bibliography

Berlin, Adele, and Marc Zvi Brettler, eds. *The Jewish Study Bible*. Oxford: Oxford University Press, 2014.

Brenton, Sir Lancelot C. L., ed. *The Septuagint with Apocrypha: Greek and English*. Grand Rapids: Zondervan, 1982.

Douglas, J. D., ed. *The New Greek-English Interlinear New Testament*. Translated by Robert K. Brown and Philip W. Comfort. Carol Stream: Tyndale, 1990.

Metzger, Bruce M., and Roland E. Murphy, eds. *The New Annotated Oxford Bible*. New York: Oxford University Press, 1991.

Morwood, James, and John Taylor, eds. *The Pocket Oxford Classical Greek Dictionary*. Oxford: Oxford University Press, 2002.

Mounce, William D. *The Analytical Lexicon to the Greek New Testament*. Grand Rapids: Zondervan, 1993.

Whitaker, Richard E., and John R. Kohlenberger III. *The Analytical Concordance to the New Revised Standard Version of the New Testament*. Grand Rapids: Eerdmans, 2000.

www.ingramcontent.com/pod-product-compliance
Lightning Source LLC
Chambersburg PA
CBHW071145090426
42736CB00012B/2234